Lars Mørch Finborud

Sanding Down Gravestones

Translated from the Norwegian
by Becky L. Crook
Except * by John Holten & Associates

Broken Dimanche Press

"To make a new horse feel comfortable. Lead it through the dining room to the dinner table. Give it something to eat."

Anton Christian Bang, *Norwegian Magic Spells and Enchantments*, 1900

WE ARE ALL ASTRONAUTS

I love all that falls, all that falls, all that falls – or – all that soars all that soars, all that soars without a thought for the pull of gravity, just before ascension or descent. And I see Buckminster Fuller smile directly into the 8mm camera and say that we are all astronauts. He swears that it's true; in this instant, the planet is falling through the universe thousands of kilometres per hour, so it's an indisputable fact – we are all astronauts.

And never is that feeling of falling or soaring, of climbing up or crashing down, stronger than when I listen to Håkon Kornstad's music. Through the last few years I've become dependent on having him in my ears as I write. I tried Steve Reich and David Axelrod. I tried Linda Perhacs and The Last Hurrah!! I tried Tony Allen and Hildur Gudnadóttir, but no one came close to Kornstad's trilogy *Single Engine, Dwell Time* and *Symphonies In My Head*, which he recorded inside Sofienberg church in Oslo between 2007 and 2011. On the first listen, the sound may seem like steadfast elevator music because it doesn't force itself on you, but builds up slowly within, like standing in the midst of a calm snowstorm just before you begin to sense the cold. The tone is so pure and sacral, almost self-destructive as it erodes in your ear, permitting you to conjure your own images and trains of thought. But concealed behind the minimalistic surface is a handful of ecstasy and doom, pitch and blood dripping from the instrument. The sound that first appeared like an Ole Sjølie painting or a Russian icon changes into a wall on which hangs three paintings with a moose in the sunset, a fisherman in a yellow sou'wester and a gipsy girl as their motifs. And in the middle of your reflections you see the girl pull out a bottle of cheap sweet wine from her crotch, the fisherman tosses his pipe into the sea, hops into her frame and goes into a convulsive jig to gain her favour as he shouts: "The sight of you makes me think of births!" And they fling themselves into the moose's painting, clamber up the bone-dry spine and in a hot impromptu act of lovemaking, ride off together into the sunset.

I love all that falls, all that falls, all that falls – or – all that soars, all that soars, all that soars, just before ascension or descent.

Why hasn't anyone used Kornstad's music as a soundtrack? The first thing I think of is the scene in the film *Oslo, August 31st* in which the main character drives out from the Ekeberg tunnel and new Oslo spreads out before his eyes. The taxi driver turns up the volume, and an a-ha tune floats from the stereo. Why didn't they use Kornstad's tones instead, the very sound of this little city so self-confidently placed atop a bedrock chock full of radon, the city that attempts to rise again after a catastrophe? Kornstad is the sound of Petter Stordalen's May 16th parties, the sound of the Enerhaug tavern where Bjørn from The Teddybearboys plays Trond Granlund's *Vaterlandsbrua* so that the entire pub sings along, the sound of a summer night filled with bumble bees, breathing windows and night bathers who bolt out of the trees around Båntjern, the sound of remedial pilsner and slot machine addicts at Frognerstranda Tavern, the sound of the grease from the pork chops that crackles on the Roma peoples' grills outside of the Botanical garden, the sound of Pløens street just after closing time, fifteen blue, snowdrifts and all the people streaming out from the bars. The sound of the ten minutes they have to find an afterparty or a one night stand before they freeze to death. The sound of summer nights in Skillebekk where me and the gang gave Dag Solstad a rude awakening in the middle of the night, held the intercom button for a long time and then ran to the garden that afforded a view directly into his bedroom. And we lay there night after night laughing ourselves sick as we watched Solstad wake up, stand confused in his underwear, pull on his robe, pad out of his bedroom into the hallway, buzz up someone who wasn't there and shake his head in defeat before hurrying to the kitchen for a glass of water where he stood for a long time glaring down at the street before turning out the light and going back to bed. Kornstad is the sound of the slow-moving cue on the E18 with one passenger per car, the quill writing on Town Hall contracts that relocate subsidized housing projects all to the same part of town, the sound of my neighbour who all his life insisted on cutting the beef length-wise and ate with such an expression that we children dubbed him Seagull, and who died at the age of 89 after inserting a piece of entrecôte in his throat. Håkon Kornstad is the sound of that summer I read Knut

Faldbakken's novel *Insect Summer* three times and believed that the Norwegian countryside was the most sexually charged place on the planet and so enlisted myself to tend pigs at Uncle Johannes' and Aunt Bjørg's farm only to discover that there wasn't a single girl my age in the entire village. Kornstad is the sound of the yearbook editor who came into our classroom at Oslo Cathedral School and wondered whether our lot had founded any new clubs that needed to be photographed? And while The Cathedral Radicals and The Cathedral Fantasy Society lined themselves up, my mate and I dashed down to the custodian's office, borrowed shovels, ran back up to the classroom and asked the photographer to come with us over to Our Saviour's Cemetery in Oslo. We stood on a gravestone, and with our shovels planted in the dirt we asked him to snap away, and when the yearbook came out, our photo had been printed, right in between The Cathedral Conservatives and The Cathedral Theatre Troupe was a photo of The Cathedral Necrophile Society. I've never seen anyone who shook with more rage than the principal as he told us what shame we had brought on the traditions of this ancient school. Kornstad's tones are the sound of Paradise Cove on the night of May 1, 1995, when we were hounded by a gang of Pakistani boys after one of us yelled: "Your mum is an astronaut" to one of them. And I thought that the offended party, who now said he was going to murder us, should rather have taken it as a compliment, but instead he stood there screaming and screaming that his mother was not an astronaut, and the only thing we could do when the gang came to take their revenge, was to wade out into Paradise Cove fully clothed, wade out so far that no rocks could hit us. And to this day I still regret not yelling in toward the shoreline where the gang stood: "You idiot, we are all astronauts, even your damned mum – just ask Buckminster Fuller!"

I love all that falls, all that falls, all that falls – or – all that soars, all that soars, that which soars just before ascension or descent. And I'm never more aware of this than when I listen to Håkon Kornstad's music.

SUICIDESOUL

On the way to work I pass an anonymous office building that houses a clinic by the name of Andrological Centre. Andrology, according to the Internet's grey voice, is the male counterpart to gynaecology, and the owner of the centre is a doctor by the name of Ken Purvis. Each time I pass, I think the name must be contrived, a clever pairing of the words pervert and penis, with the sole aim to penetrate the subconscious of male clients. Purvis – one should get paid a dirt allowance just to put the word in your mouth. And perhaps it was a peripheral peer of Purvis who called me in one day in ninth grade at Ruseløkka School. Together with Ebbe, another thin stick-figure without an ounce of fat on his body, I was instructed to visit the school's combined dental and medicinal clinic. Once inside we were informed that the Oslo school health officials had launched a new programme to hinder the abnormal growth of tall young men in the capital city. The doctor said that based on my height of 180 cm at only the age of 15, there was a real chance that I was going to be unusually tall as an adult. He asked whether I knew that people over two metres five were defined as sick, on par with overweight and those with spinal problems? Fortunately, with the help of new medicines, one could hinder that from happening now. I had only to pull my trousers down to my knees so that he could check my testicles to see how far along into puberty I'd come. He pulled on a pair of rubber gloves, opened a yellow and green jar of vaseline, lubricated my balls, squeezed gently on certain points and took out a metal ruler to measure the circumference. Then he tore a bit of paper towel from a large industrial roll, polished the goo from my scrotum, and said I could cinch up my trousers again. Ebbe sat in the waiting room trying to make eye contact. I stared down at the blue, marbleised linoleum.

When the letter arrived from the health officials, my mum walked right into the TV room and woke dad from his midday nap. The test results indicated that there was a high likelihood that my body was going to grow considerably over the following years. At the end of my development I would reach around 220 centimetres in my socks. Based on my present height, and the fact that my testicles were less advanced, the doctor suggested a mild steroid treatment so that my body would grow more outward than upward. Mum and dad asked me to leave the room and shut the door. I lay on my bed and stared in turns out the window at the carnivorous climbing plant in our backyard and the poster of Freddy Krüeger on the side of my closet. "In a few years I'm going to be a monster like you, Freddy. I'll have to sneak into the school at night, borrow the saw from woodworking and cut off my legs at the knees. There must be some kind of shoes I can fasten on the blunt stumps, once the wounds have healed, maybe those kind of round tennis shoes that Huey, Dewey and Louie wear around in Duckburg?" Mum and dad came into my bedroom, sat on the edge of my bed, and informed me that I shouldn't worry about the letter: "Nature will have its course, we shouldn't meddle with it." They would love me even if I became taller than the tallest man alive, prime minister, plumber or arborist, and tonight we weren't going to eat at home, but cross the bridge to Frognerstranda Tavern to get a burger with fries. My future as a monster was hereby called off. I grew to 1,93 high without using steroids. Ebbe went on the treatment and his shoulders grew a bit wider, but he landed around 1,90 as well.

Fifteen years later, we're standing at the top of the diving tower at Ingierstrand Bath. Ebbe and I. It's an early Tuesday morning and there's not a soul in sight, apart from two cats helping themselves to the charred remains of an extinguished barbecue. We have slept terribly the last weeks and it's no exaggeration to claim that life is tearing at us. We are out of sync, but have decided to take up the struggle, by beginning each day with an early dawn swim at chosen locations in the Oslo fjord. You drive in your dirty, red Mazda down along Hagegata and after a few muffled words through the window, realize that you haven't come down from the previous day. You are overtired and drunk, so I ask you to drive slowly down Mosseveien. Sometimes you step on the gas just to fuck with me, we have so much to do, you wish to show me the joys of Follo county! Roald Amundsen's house in the village of Svartskog, breakfast at Villa Sandvigen and perhaps a remedial pint at Tyrigrava Tavern, if they're still open. But first the morning swim.

We can't bring ourselves to jump. The problem is that it's even scarier to descend the ladder again. When we were kids, we jumped from the same heights at Panter'n and Frogner public bath without batting an eye, but now we both weigh over a hundred kilos and the slap when we hit the water will be colossal – our subcutaneous fat and stretch marks are going to howl in unison. That's when you throw out your suggestion; if we take off our pants and throw them into the water, we will be forced to retrieve them, otherwise we'll face the unforgiving punishment of streaking all the way up to the parking lot. Two pairs of underwear sail outward from the ten metre. My coarse cotton underwear gets waterlogged and sink, while your leopard print silk pair drift away with the Oslo fjord current; they must be rescued, now or never. That is when you look me in the eyes and ask: "Have you ever thought about taking your life, Lars?" And then you take two quick steps and cast yourself out with all your strength. I'm certain you've hopped to the wrong side, toward the rocks, but over the edge I see you in flight toward the fjord. Afraid that you aren't planning to surface again, I hop out to the left so as not to land on you. But no rescue operation is necessary, in midair I see your head emerge from the body of water, and then you release the worst howl I've ever heard. At first I can't comprehend what you're screaming, but then the words reach me clearly: "Hold your testicles, hold your testicles, hold your testicles, Lars!" I form my hands into a pink shield and hit the water.

You're barely able to drive to Tyrikleiva: one hand on your balls; one hand on the wheel. I say that I could have driven, but you know I don't have my license, so I'm relegated as usual to the role of selecting the music. There's a stack of burned CDs on a spindle in the glove compartment. I inappropriately take out a disc on which *Suicidesoul* has been scrawled with a black marker, it's a genre we made up to describe soul music that sounds like the vocalist is on the verge of taking his own life to reside on the ocean floor. I feed the disk into the player and as we drive along Gamle Mossevei, the sound of Kenny Wells' song *I Can't Stop* streams from the player.

You are far soberer now. I would like to start a conversation, cheerful or not. Should I tell you that I once found a plant here, a Eupatorium, called *hjortetrøst* in Norwegian, meaning "the solace of deer", and I thought it was so ineffably beautiful that our ancestors came up with a name like that? Or should I rail on about how the city has incontrovertibly gone from smelling like dog faeces to stinking of human excrement, and that I read a lot of meaning into that? I sit mutely as the next tune fades in on the mix. I recognize it immediately. It's Willie West & The High Society Brothers' *The Devil Gives Me Everything*, also known as the world's saddest song, a harsh winter of a life in three minutes. Should I go on about how messed up it is that people are so careful about washing their hands after pissing, but that they suck and lick their lovers at night until they get a gold medal – we all suffer from hygienic behavioural problems? Or that when you drive a car and gaze out at the vast landscape along the motorway, there's a trembling sense of evil that's present...? No, it's easier to pull down the sun than to change your mood, there's no mustering your enthusiasm. I turn up the volume and listen to the suicidesoul.

ANYTHING AT ALL BY GUNNAR EKELÖF

I own a jutegnask. A soul-filled relic that floats in a vague no-man's-land between art and rubbish. Picture Meredith Monk's doormat. Harald Szeeman's dirty napkin. Jean Genet's used bath towel. Harry Bertoia's toothpick. I know that most people who collect jutegnask will make the same claim, but mine is the best jutegnask in the world. The index card reads:

> STIG SÆTERBAKKEN'S LITERATURE RECOMMENDATIONS (2001)
> A list of ten novels, ten short story collections, ten essay collections and ten poetry collections which Stig Sæterbakken thinks one ought to read before the age of 21.
>
> A4 page with printed black ink
> G- (visible coffee stains, paper structure broken)
> LMFJG0001

In 1999, based on my reading of Fyodor Dostoevsky's *Crime and Punishment*, I was offered a job at an institution for patients with double diagnoses. Even though the job description called for a candidate who had completed their social work education studies and with a minimum age of 25,

I was nonetheless able to convince them over the phone that a nineteen-year-old with a vague familiarity with Russian literature was equally qualified. After a few months I was tired of attack dogs with bad stomachs and the sashaying offers for sex from 31-year-old drug legends – I dreamed about working at a mail sorting facility far away from people. Two months after the deadline, I applied to the literature programme at the Nansen School in Lillehammer. I was told by the receptionist to send the application, an aggressive motivational letter and five *Baudelaire in Norwegian*-prose poems direct to Stig Sæterbakken, who had recently been hired as the head teacher. Shortly thereafter, Stig called me up to inform me that I could be a student in his class on one condition: I had to make my own living arrangements, since the school's residence halls were full. That made two of us that year. Stig himself was also roaming about Lillehammer like a shabby bear, refusing to get a trim until he was able to find a permanent home for his family. A housing crisis in Gudbrandsdalen was required for me to finally become a student of Sæterbakken in his first and last year as head teacher for the literature programme at the Nansen School. He needed the money as much as he detested paperwork and meetings.

It's never a good sign to realize that your life has become like a discarded Christopher Nielsen comic strip, but in the course of the year in Lillehammer, virgins lost their titles in all kinds of ways, the portent of petit-nihilism stood above us, and at the parties you could be certain there would always be some aspiring writer with a knife who loudly announced to everyone in the room that that if you wished to commit suicide, you had to cut your wrist vertically, not horizontally. He'd have read his Bjørneboe. When a friend blew his head off with an elephant rifle, the atmosphere was dampened. Stig made the year worth it. He was encouraging and ruthless in his reception of all the fumbling attempts and recommended literature to each and every one of the students, based on their personalities. He dragged us from our beds if we didn't show up at the morning lectures, truly outraged, even though he had been out with us the night before. Thank god Stig didn't become a man of the church.

After Lillehammer, I went to Dublin to study the history of philosophy and art, but didn't want to give up literature completely. At the General Post Office in O'Connell Street, I sent off a bottle of Irish whiskey and added a letter to Stig asking him for a list with books that a young man should read before turning 21. Scared to death that the bottle would break, I wrapped it in a wool sock, and then duct-tape, another wool sock, duct-tape, and then plastic bags, duct-tape, then a torn up t-shirt, duct-tape and finally an address label affixed on the outside. Some weeks later, an envelope addressed to me lay on the kitchen table. It contained a thank you from Stig for the whiskey and told that he has spent half an hour freeing the bottle, but assured me it had been well worth it. Attached was also an A4 size page with 40 obligatory books divided into four categories "10 NOVELS, 10 SHORT STORY COLLECTIONS, 10 ESSAY COLLECTIONS, 10 POETRY COLLECTIONS" it said in all caps.

A decade later, I uncovered the list when I was moving my belongings from my father's basement. With its fitting coffee stains and scar-like folds the page looked like a fake, as if someone had tried to falsify a document to mimic something timeless. Authors such as Genet, Bernhard, Céline, Strindberg, Miller, Handke, Bataille, Cortázar and Celan were named – who wouldn't end up as a perverse aspiring writer if he'd read such names before turning 21? As I sat in the basement, I began to think about where I had read those books, their characters and the assignments I'd had. Apart from its high sentimental value, the list bore the mark of uncompromising quality, roaring laughter and candour, love for and a dependence on literature. I read and read and read, until the timer switch turned off the light in the basement. I turned on my mobile phone and studied the small details on the page in the half-light:

> Odd Klippenvåg – Expectations and Redemptions (particularly the title piece)
> Raymond Carver (anything he's written, as a study of the modern American short story, which is the model for 99% of today's Norwegian short story writers).
> Gunnar Ekelöf (anything at all)

Anything at all by Gunnar Ekelöf.

In recent years, I've come across Stig in fits and starts. In 2008 he appeared together with the Christian Wallumrød Ensemble at the Henie Onstad Kunstsenter where I work, and he sent us his last essay to the catalogue following the artist Per Inge Bjørlo's 2011 exhibition. When he was going to read with Wallumrød, he asked me to send over the music ahead of time, just to be sure that The Preservation Hall Brass Band wasn't going to come marching in on the stage as he read. I sent off two of Wallumrød's albums, and a few days later an email popped up from Stig with *Sad Music* in the subject line.

> Hi Lars,
> I got the CDs today.
> Am traveling to the Isle of Islay tonight, a pilgrimage to whiskeyland, but am taking Wallumrød on my iPod, which is to say that I will give you a clear answer when I get back home: if it's sad enough, I'll say yes, Sunday evening.
> Best, Stig

On Sunday, I received a new email. It *was* sad music. He agreed.

Stig had a well developed grave instinct. But he also had an over developed heart. This jutegnask serves as a memory of a good teacher and friend, and a small contribution to the debate about future readings lists. From one jutegnask collector to all you others.

COLOURED PEOPLE

It's the jumble sale at Vålerenga School. For once I've arrived early, but several eager people are crowded behind a red rope that will be cut when the clock strikes ten. The mood is slightly chaotic and there's no clear queuing system, a few individuals attempt to lure some of the marching band volunteers on the other side of the rope to tell them where things are located in order to secure a flying start. A young Somalian couple joins this expectant, but easily-frustrated company of thrift seekers and treasure hunters. They commit the unpardonable sin of jumping the queue and one man is so outraged that he screams out, "Hey, stop there, you coloured people!" It now becomes evident that they have tried to jump the queue in front of none other than the wretch of all wretches, the everyday hero of everyday heroes, the opinionated watchdog of the daily life's immensely varied and luxurious period of fertility. When the couple fails to respond to his insult, the man takes it upon himself to offer them a lecture on Norwegian etiquette. He preaches at them in English and delivers his sermon on the mount at a bellow: "A wise American man by the name of John F. Kennedy once said: it's not about what your country can do for you, but what you can do for your country." The mood is, to put it mildly, tense. I think that if the guy had an ounce of wit between his ears, he might realize that the Somalian couple isn't out to snatch the same Junipher Greene LP or the same Grete Prytz Kittelsen platter, they don't look like experts on Scandinavian progrock or modern enamel handicrafts from the 1950s. The day is saved when a girl from the marching band cuts the rope and the wretch sees his chance to run like the dickens to get ahead first.

The Saturday evening news broadcasts a report from the large jumble sale in Oslo. They've also been to Vålerenga and set up cameras to film what they dub "the jumble sale fever ravaging our country". The feature depicts our everyday hero bounding up the stairs, bolting down several corridors and into the gymnasium to the boxes of records where he tries to finagle them into a square so as to have first dibs on everything. He hadn't quite anticipated that the jumble sale would be broadcast to over a million people, but that fact hardly seems to bother him. As the reporter attempts to extract a comment, he flips through stacks of LPs with Bert Kaempfert and *Svensktoppar* and discovers a flawless copy of Karin Krog and Steve Kuhn's album *We Could Be Flying* from 1975. The wretch emits a small "holy shit" for Saturday news viewers, before telling the reporter, his voice aquiver, that so much hard work goes into this digging, but it's these kind of instances, when you find nuggets like this, that make the entire thing, for one fleeting moment, worth all the toil.

I press mute on the remote and walk over to the banana box in the living room to find my own worn out copy of the album. As I'm leafing through the pile, I remember that there is an album with Monica Zetterlund, *Chicken Feathers*, that contains the same Kuhn-compositions that are on *We Could Be Flying*. Why didn't I think of that when I watched the new Oedipus-tainted Zetterlund film a few days ago? Of course it's Kuhn who is portrayed as the unfaithful character Steve Chambers. Monica dreams of becoming one of those old married couples who worry about walking up hills in the winter, but Kuhn abandons her. I also have in my collection a live recording of Steve Kuhn playing his own compositions on Buddah Records which is superior to the two Scandinavian versions. I think the secret is that Kuhn's voice dwells in that span between a cool Chet Baker-tone bathed in neon light, and a man who is so befuddled and awful at singing that, in desperation, he finally, with every little muscle in his palate or tongue, tries maintaining a pure tone. Gary McFarland's arrangements for string are not accompanied by any weather advisories and paint up storms that swell in over the land of Andante. I pull out the vinyl and put on my favourite track, *The Meaning of Love.*

The needle has slipped out of the grooves and onto the label, I must have dozed off on the sofa, as so often happens these days. On the other side of Åkebergveien I see a light pressed out through the frosted windowpanes at the Botsen prison as I pour a glass full of whiskey. It must be windy out, the street light suspended between the prison and building of flats swings about, casting a frail disco light onto the living room wall. As the crow flies, there are fewer than twelve metres between me and an imprisoned person. Sitting at my writing desk and gazing down at the prison, I have comic book fantasies, I picture a mastermind criminal sitting in his cell sending out high frequency impulses through the airwaves and taking over my brain. I often look to see whether the orange doors of the bare cells are open or shut, the only sign of life. I turn my gaze toward the visitors entrance where families and friends stand waiting just before eight o'clock. Each and every one on their best behaviour on the way in, but they don't know what to do with themselves when they come out again. On other days, newly released prisoners sit on the steps with a large, brown envelope beside them and perform a quick change of clothes. They must been allowed to change on the inside, before they were released, but most likely they want to get out the door as quickly as possible. Sometimes a friend is waiting just outside with a needle. They can't wait, and scuffle around the corner only meters away from the entrance, fall asleep beneath the security cameras. The prison guards come running out and don't know what they should do with them.

When I was a child, a man stood in our fireplace at home. One day, two filthy feet sank slowly down from the chimney and landed suddenly in the soot. At times, that uninvited guest was my best conversational partner, even if he only shuffled around in the soot in response to my questions. As an adult, the man in the fireplace has been replaced by the man in custody. I tell him about the couple on the bus this morning, from whom I could not remove my gaze. The man was short and stout with incandescent carrot-coloured skin, a pronounced chin and a slick crew cut. She had an attractive, anxiety-inducing appearance; everything was in place, but not in a way that made any sense. I thought it must be the carrot man who was fulfilling his Frankenstein dreams by forcing her to snip here and cut there for his visionary lusts. But in the next second, I was certain that she – poor woman – must be in the middle of a recovery period following a mutilating car accident or harrowing cancer, and that they must both be on their way to the hospital. As you can see, I'm unable to decide on anything. From along Åkebergveien float sounds of partygoers on their way to the city from Kampen and Galgeberg. It reminds me of the noise when you all have football matches at the jail on Sunday evenings and the footpaths outside the prison walls are thick with guards. Must you all boast so loudly? Even the police cars with their flashing lights wait to turn on their sirens until they've swung out into Kjølbergata, thereby saving us neighbours from the nuisance. The only reason that Oslo has a jail in its centre is not that the city's more or less law-abiding citizens should constantly be reminded of the existence of the law enforcement agencies. It is rather so that you convicts should be forced to hear the continuous sounds of life passing beyond the walls, an extra punishment. For the first time, you are given a one room flat in the city centre but you're not even allowed to walk out the door. To offer some words of consolation to someone who is locked in: those who are now going out on the town, wake more often to bits of kebab between their teeth than to the taste of pussy after a late night. Sperm in one's naval from jerking off the night before happens much more often the next day than traces of wet, meaningful kisses on your neck. Pardon my use of language, but I'm assuming that, like most convicts, you're a hopeless masturbator, or more correctly, in not too long, a skinless masturbator. I myself have sat in a bare cell and know that the trick for coping with the time is to wank yourself unconscious until your term is up. Wank off until your prick looks like a dog's dick put through a rusty pencil sharpener, that's when both your consciousness and the punishment disappear. And if that's not comforting enough, imagine that you're not completely impounded, not really. I've seen a person who truly was. Are you listening? On the farm neighbouring our family cabin, a worker threw himself directly into the fish net that had been hung to dry in the barn. He floundered and twisted, becoming increasingly more entangled in the fish net, writhing violently until the thin strands cut off his blood circulation. Me and some other children had the honour of finding him hanging from the roof. We thought a spider must have trapped him in its web and looked in alarm around us. Blue clumps of skin oozed out between threads, reminding me of when Aunt Idun twist-squeezed the towel that had been used to filter out the berry flesh when she would make blue berry juice. Now that's prison.

Did I tell you about that wretch that I saw at the jumble sale today? There wasn't a good bone in his body – he quoted Kennedy in English and behaved like a complete oaf toward a Somalian couple who he feared was going to cheat him out of some flea market find. I collect wretches, so even though it's late, I must tell you about my favourite wretch. I discovered him in a documentary by the name of *The Seven Executioners,* or something to that effect. It's about a film crew that travels around Europe and the USA interviewing people who, at some point in their careers have held the professional title: *executioner*. They travel to Serbia, where one former executioner begins to sob and wants to turn around the car as they near the wooded area where he participated in executing three Muslim policemen. In Romania, we meet an executioner who peppered Mr and Mrs Ceausescu with four hundred shots until they looked like melted snowmen in April. According to him, he was hired twenty minutes before the execution and was obviously bitter about what appears to have been a clear violation of the executioner's labour rights – all 20 of the rifles were loaded with ammunition, no blanks. And in this way, the film topic digs up individuals with large, wet Nürnberg eyes in every nook and cranny of Europe. Finally, they travel to the USA and find the wretch I wish to mention. He is an old man with an even older cat at his side, whose meow is so shrill and who shuffles around so loudly on his petrified claws that he has to be thrown out of the room where the interview is being conducted. The elderly gentleman is a former American soldier who was appointed to execute Hermann Göring. Since Göring was able to commit suicide in his cell with a cyanide capsule, he never fulfilled his task. The man appears as a warm grandfatherly figure, but the bubble of illusion bursts when the interviewer asks how it felt when Göring escaped his due punishment: "When a prisoner who is waiting to be executed manages to commit suicide, it's the worst thing that can happen to an executioner. I've often thought about how I would have liked to slice open some wounds down his back, to poke at them a bit, so that he could feel more pain." The interview continues with questions about other executions that the wretch has in fact fulfilled, before he interrupts. "Have you seen the photo? *The* photo?" The interviewer indicates that he doesn't know which photo the wretch is talking about. "Proof!" The old man takes out a tiny photograph and shows it to the camera. A black and white image shows Adolf Hitler standing atop a submarine together with two young girls with sacks of money under each arm. The photo is dated May 3, 1945. "They went to Atlantis. We didn't get the better of him either."

It's almost four o'clock. I have the feeling you're no longer listening. I stand and walk over to the turntable, spin the vinyl and set the needle down on *Pearlies Swine*. Poor ol' Steve Kuhn opens his maw and rouses up his dark lyrics:

Send twenty dollars to me
So I can be free
To see
How birds eat their food in the trees

Ham
How I love to eat ham
Vultures don't give a damn

Meat
Monkeys eat with their feet

So that when I'm alone
Left with only a bone
On top of the sky
Birds are wondering why.

AN ARNE NORDHEIM LOOK-ALIKE

You start to laugh when you see the first mock-up of the T-shirt for the Nordheim exhibition that I'm curating at Henie Onstad Kunstsenter. I ask what's so funny, and you point at the photo of a young Arne Nordheim wearing horn rimmed glasses that is going to be silk screened across the chest: "You look completely alike, the only thing you're missing is a comb-over, but you'll have that soon enough. It's going to seem pretty meta with you walking around in that shirt at the exhibiton." When your laughter has died down, you offer to start making dinner since I still have so much work to do. I reply as usual that I only have about a half hour left.

I've spent my entire workday transcribing citations from old newspaper clippings and VHS cassettes. I've been hunting for Nordheim quotations to cut out with a vinyl cutter plotter and paste up along the exhibition wall. Throughout my search I have pondered how a composer who wrote such gravely good compositions like *Greening* and *Dinosaurus*, and who created such monolithic installations like *Dråpen* (The Drop) and *Ode til lyset* (Ode to The Light), could in the same breath be such a great pedagogue. In my hand I am holding a newspaper clipping from 1955 with the headline *Young killjoy laughs at his own funeral march,* in which the journalist asks a 24-year-old Arne Nordheim: "What about the present, the past and -isms?" The young composer, who had just debuted in Copenhagen with the work *Epigram for String Quartet* replies confidently: "No -isms for me, thanks!" I write that down.

Scrolling down the word document, I see that I've selected far too many citations. It's impossible to choose, I'm easily dazzled by Nordheim's rich vocabulary, but first and foremost by his ability to formulate difficult, artistic challenges in such a straightforward way. The first quotes are:

> I am death and catastrophe – you may call me hardcore.

> I view technology with the grandest romantic delight.

> Dylan Thomas said: "An artist's place is to fall between several chairs." And in my field, I must add, "And at least one of them should be electric."

> Worst of all is for art to be called mild.

> Helge Sten has stated that Arne Nordheim is superb. He must be an exceptionally wise man.

After some back and forth, I cross out the last quote.

The Arne Nordheim documentary from 1974, *Occupation: Composer* is a honeypot of quotes into which I happily stick my paw. The film opens with Nordheim running around in some hair-raising

Marimekko bell-bottoms with vertical red and white stripes as he trumpets:

> Many people believe that we composers who live and work today wish only to blow to pieces tradition and anything that's safe. But an explosion does not release us from the thoughts and feelings that other people have lived and felt before our time... I myself often feel like a proper old-fashioned country composer, a sleepy romantic with no ulterior motives, neither with regard to dairy farming or the cultural revolution.

In the next scene, he spins, scurries and dances around Eila Hiltunen's Sibelius monument in Helsinki as his voiceover explains:

> Being within the sound, that is what it is to be a composer. I wish to enter into the sound, I would like to hear inside of the sheet of iron, I would like to hear inside of the clock, I would like enter into the organ.

Occupation: Composer ends with Nordheim sitting in his composer cave with a utility knife in one hand and a Mahler record in the other. He proceeds to scratch it up forcefully. Then he puts the record onto the gramophone and listens to the sound of his destruction. I re-read the quote that follows this scene over and over again:

> I think that music reaches down to the plane where it meets Man in a place I would call: Man is utterly alone. Because I think that we are all alone. And it's

> only when one descends, has been able to dig past all of the layers of profit, materialism, when one gets down there, that there begins to be a fellowship in the loneliness, and that is what I as a composer have seen and understood, that if I am going to continue on, I must be honest with myself, because I am the first listener. I am the first who at the most basic level is trying out my music on people. I am a part of everyone else, and if I don't write the music that takes hold of me, I have a feeling that I've failed. That I've failed everyone else who is also me.

I realize that Nordheim wasn't writing to change this world, but to save himself. But what's even better, he did it with a gleam in his eye, because his eleventh commandment was that one should not bore one's audience. And I think about how my generation is so saturated by concepts and distance, that when a 50-year-old man with a comb-over talks about the basic feelings of humans, about death, longing, catastrophes and love – with sincerity in his voice – that it sounds more refreshing than anything else in contemporary music and art.

A knock at the door. I ask if you are here to tease the Arne Nordheim clone, but you just want to inform me that dinner is ready. During the meal I try to push Nordheim out of my head by taking up an ongoing conversation we've been having this week. One morning before work as we were lying in bed pressing snooze to delay getting up, you asked if I was able to list the things that meant the most for me in life. You were either very sure about your case, or else you wanted to go before me, because your list sounded determined: "Number 1: to swim in the ocean. Number 2: To wake up next to you. Number 3: To spend time outdoors and watch things grow." I explain that there are so many things in life that I love, and that three things is too few, five or ten are also lacking. You ask me to try anyway, and I start off limpingly: "To have enough time to buy, prepare and eat food. To listen to music that claws at and does something to me. To arrive in a city and attack it for the first time. To put down an image or a sentence that I have had circling in my head for a long time onto a piece of paper and to see it stick. To hang out with family and godchildren. To work so extremely hard that your body and head can't take any more, but to know that you have a long summer vacation ahead of you so you push yourself just a bit harder. To not get out of bed but to watch five or six films in a row in order to dream about the films throughout the night." You interrupt me to say that I have come up with seven things, I have to whittle it down to three. I don't know, my uncertainty plagues me, I have no simple answer as to what makes me happy or unhappy. Some days I wake and love everything around me, and anything at all is good enough. Simply eating yoghurt with fresh blueberries or meeting an old acquaintance can feel like heaven, while on other days I have such an over-developed tendency to be grave that nothing seems to work. I'm sorry, it's impossible to map out all that's best in the world, but I promise to try again tomorrow. I thank you for the meal, walk into the living room and put on a piece that transforms me into a slightly more whole human. Arne Nordheim's *Solitaire* streams from the loud speakers.

LISTEN TO THE SILENCE – JOHN CAGE AS POET, MUSHROOM LOVER AND ANARCHIST

Not many composers have left behind a considerable production within other art forms than music. John Milton Cage Jr. (1912—1992) is one of the few. His artistic oeuvre includes sound poetry, lithographs and water colour paintings, abstract mushroom cookbooks, theatre plays in graphic notation, mesostic poems and socio-philosophical texts, all accentuated by principles stemming from Cage's work as a musical composer. Morton Feldman has said that if Duchamp rescued the head from the eyes, Cage rescued the ears from the head.[1] But Cage's *Happy New Ears*-utopia, which would liberate music from man-made traditions in order to try and return it back to nature, contained a method that he thought could be utilized in all arts forms. Eventually this could liberate every single human being, resulting in a utopian-anarchistic society.

In 1951 Cage visited an anechoic chamber, a completely sound isolated room constructed for research into hearing impairments and acoustics. In theory this room, located at Harvard University, would accommodate absolute silence, but Cage maintained that he could hear the sound of his nervous system quivering and his blood being pumped around his body, coming to a simple conclusion: there is no such thing as silence. Even in silence, there is sound.

Silence had in the past been defined as a pause in between other sounds within a system of sounds and to which little musical intention was ascribed. Cage however, after his experience in the anechoic chamber, was convinced of the falsity of this point of view: there was no silence in music, only a different form of music, and it was this music, that is the pauses, the silence, that Cage made into his artistic basis. By liberating this silence from the musical system and any underlying artistic intentions, he wanted to create a new music. Cage gave silence the same status as music and claimed that if only one listened, one would hear that all sound is music.

In his compositions Cage attempted to set free sounds, let them be themselves and not be fettered by systems, historical references or artistic feelings. The sounds of his music were not to be placed as signs in musical notation. Throughout history, European music, and German music in particular, centred around the construction of systems and traditions to tame the phonetic chaos one finds in nature. To Cage this was nothing more than an attempt to limit the human ability to experience sound. He wished to go in the opposite direction. Cage wanted music to imitate nature, in which change, chaos and accidents are the leading principles, and to open up music and the audience's faculty of perception to these uncontrollable variables. This demanded new compositional techniques, as well as for the audience to forget all those accepted aesthetic categories and expectations which only serve to obstruct the experience of this new music.

Although Cage had the Californian-based, Austrian composer Arnold Schönberg as mentor – a relationship based on Cage's promise of full dedication to the music, in return for which he would receive free lessons – Cage stated that he was anti-German. It is not therefore particularly surprising that his theories are based on characteristically American ideas. He garnered ideas from American pragmatists, like Charles Sanders Pierce and John Dewey with their notion that experience is art/art is experience, the function of art thus being 'that of recovering the continuity of aesthetic experience with normal processes of living'[2]. Cage was inspired by Walt Whitman's absolute democratic heritage in which everything that belongs to our perceptible reality is entitled to an equal amount of attention. As a good West Coast American Cage's gaze was fixed squarely on the Pacific Ocean rather than on the Atlantic. Towards the end of the 1940s Cage studied Indian philosophy under Gita Sarabhai and Zen Buddhism under Daisetz T. Suzuki at Columbia University, in which he found the idea of letting things, humans and sounds be themselves. Moreover he became convinced that alteration is the fundamental principle of reality and that reality thus must be understood as a process rather than a state of being. Cage's self-proclaimed 'anti-Germanness', however, can be taken with a pinch of salt. Even if they were to be used for fundamentally different ends, there is something acutely Germanic about his insistence on the hard working artist and emphasis on intellect and concentration.

Developing ideas from Luigi Russolo and Edgar Varèses on the introduction of sounds from everyday life into musical language and notation, Cage wrote in his first music manifesto, *The Future of Music: Credo* (1940) that we are moving towards an 'all-sound' music. Considering that every single sound finds its value in itself, all sounds are welcome in music, and Cage's innovations, such as the employment of prepared piano, recorders and electronic instruments, were a consequence of this. When noise is equal to Lutheran chorale, slapping a car tyre generates just a good a sound as a Stradivarius violin. Being a faithful student of his mentor Schönberg, Cage removed all tonal and harmonic structures from his compositions. For Cage this was not a question of finding alternative and looser systems such as the twelve tone system, but rather an attempt to move towards an equally free and coincidental music such as that found in nature. Being an artist was no longer a question of imposing one's ego, inner pain or virtuosity on the audience, but rather a question of what the composer, the performer and the audience could rather create together. Cage's definition of art became 'a process set in motion by a group of people', a definition that was to be important to subsequent art forms such as happenings and events and to the general shift in art towards multimedia and performance. Importantly Cage did not view these new and modern art forms fashionable, rebellious or as experimental, but as necessary steps to de-instrumentalise the fixed human mode of perception: "One does not then make just any experiment but does what must be done"[3]

Cage started composing by posing questions: *What kinds of tempi? Which sounds? What about the duration of the pauses?* Cage answered this questioning by introducing so-called chance operations into his modes of composition. These were inspired by methods found in the 5000-year-old Chinese text *I Ching,* the reader of which could have questions answered by throwing yarrow stalks – or in Cage's case, dice – that generated a number which would refer to one of the 64 different oracle hexagrams in the book. In this way Cage discovered a method for creating art without intentions or artistic pretensions, a method more radical than that of the automatism of the Surrealists, because this method allowed for composition to occur beyond the realm of the self. It was Cage's belief that music composed following this method – his first being *Music of Changes* written for David Tudor in 1951 – would lead to an acceptance of things in themselves and give precedence to an immediate and irreducible experience.

Although composed by using the role of chance, Cage gradually discovered that the performance of his pieces and notations were as determined as any work of Beethoven's. Following on from his theory of the constant flux and changing nature of all things, the next step for Cage was to introduce a concept of indeterminacy into his music. Cage began to compose pieces consisting of graphic notations and written directions, making the pieces so open that they would be subject to change and alteration with every single performance. A clear example of this was *Indeterminacy*[4] in which Cage read humorous anecdotes in one room and David Tudor played in another, without the two of them being able to hear each other. Likewise *Imaginary Landscape No. 4,* a piece for twelve radios whose frequency and volume the performer would control, but with each performance the radios inevitably picking up different signals.

The most famous piece embracing the idea of indeterminacy is *4'33"*. On the original performance of the piece, on August 29, 1952 in Woodstock, David Tudor sat by a grand piano for 4:33 minutes (a time span determined by the use of *I Ching* chance operations) and did not touch a single key. His only movements during the performance were three waves of his hand marking the commencement of new sections. According to the legend the windows of the concert hall were wide open, letting in the sounds of the pouring rain outside. This underlined the extreme openness of the piece: accidental sounds emerging at a given time and place, if not to say the spatiotemporal circumstances themselves, during the course the piece's performance, all become integral parts of the piece. Although possibly altered in order to point toward Cage's later work which was often written for outdoor performance which would be at the mercy of the weather gods and meteorological coincidences, the story of the first performance of *4'33"* serves to highlight how the work only becomes meaningful in the active interaction between medium, performer and audience and the common experience this interaction creates. After the concert, you were not to walk home with a new tune to whistle or with your aesthetic preferences fulfilled but rather with a richer sensibility – and eventually, a richer understanding of the world.

JOHN CAGE'S MESOSTIC POETRY

During the 1950s, due to rheumatism in his hands, Cage directed his artistic activities more towards the written word. Cage saw it as his artistic charge to introduce elements belonging to one art form into other art forms. At an early stage he pointed out the similarities between composing music and writing poetry. According to Cage the musical base elements, time and sound, are more prominent in poetry than in prose.

An art form that was to remain important to Cage all throughout his life was his so called 'Lectures', in which he textualised the ideas and modes of composition that he employed in his music. *Lecture on Nothing* from 1950 is for instance written within the same rhythmic structure as his piece *Sonatas and Interludes,* and *London Lecture* from the same year is written with the use of chance operations. Cage's 'Lectures' have many of the same qualities as his early percussion music and pieces for the prepared piano: anti- syntactical, peculiar sound textures, quick changes in tempo and theme, as well as erratic pauses. When asked by the poet M.C. Richards why he wouldn't just hold a normal lecture, as this would shock the audience even more than another experimental lecture, Cage replied "I don't give these lectures to surprise people, but out of the need for poetry."[5]

Another text form Cage was to work on extensively was that of the personal journal in his 'Diaries', poetic in its form, written in the years between 1965 and 1982 and published under the Zen Buddhist title of *Diary: How to Improve the World (You Will Only Make Matters Worse)*. Cage used the constant flow of occurrences, texts, newspaper articles and ideas in his everyday life as sources, treating them with his postmodern lawnmower that rearranged this material into a form of poetic mosaic. The idea of change as the fundamental principle of nature led Cage to an extensive use of other people's texts as source material. The material was not sampled in order to provide information or lend it credibility. By writing himself through the prism of other people's texts, Cage demonstrated that these texts could be used to create brand new texts as well as ideas.

In *Diaries* Cage again donned the monk's robe and began to ask questions: 'Which parts of the texts will I use?' 'Where do I start the poem?' 'How many minuscules will I use in the third line?' Then he would consult *I Ching* and the results were the highly original anti-syntactical and unstructured poems to be found in *Diaries*. In the same vein as his attempt to liberate sounds from musical structures, Cage now tried to liberate the word from the structure of language. *Diaries* intimate the entirely anti-syntactical language which Cage was to move toward in his later text pieces, *Mureau* and *Muoyce* and in his collection of poetry *Empty Words*[6] where the words were just that: empty and void of meaning or intention. As a means to approach the indeterminate in poetry, Cage also introduced visual elements into his poems. Just as in his music he had removed himself from traditional harmonies and used graphic notations and written directions, Cage now began to utilize several different fonts, sizes and formatting that he found on his IBM type writer: italics, underlining, bold. Such visual manifestation made it hard to read the same poem in the same way twice.

His preferred poetic form however, Cage discovered only by coincidence when he wrote a birthday greeting to critic Edwin Denby[7], in which he outlined Denby's name in capital letters wherever they happened to appear in the text.

> rEmembering a Day i visited you -- seems noW
> as I write that the weather theN was warm -- i
> recall nothing we saiD, nothing wE did; eveN so
> (perhaps Because of that) that visit staYs.

This technique was to form the basis for the development of Cage's distinctive poetical form, *mesostics*, in which a name or theme word are highlighted in capital letters running vertically down the body of the poem. Mesostics is different from *acrostics*, where the name or word in capital letters runs down the left margin of the poem, employed by poets such as Lewis Carroll and Jackson Mac Low.[8] The spine of capital letters in mesostics gave Cage a starting point, or an oracle as he termed it himself, that enabled him to solve the poems like he solved a jigsaw. Cage distinguished two types of mesostics: 50% mesostics in which between the capital letters there are only minuscule letters, and 100% mesostics in which there is not only minuscule letters in between capital letters but minuscule rows not containing the particular capital letters which they are placed between. Before he died, Cage produced hundreds of mesostics, in which names and words such as James Joyce, Marcel Duchamp, Merce Cunningham, Erik

Satie, Ezra Pound, Ben Weber, Mushrooms and Indeterminacy formed the spine. In the mesostics *Writing for the Second Time through Finnegans Wake*, the name JAMES JOYCE ran down the poem as a spine. Finnegans Wake was used as a source text to find words which contain the letters in the name. Listing these words he used chance operations in order to determine which words he was to use and where they were to be placed. Eventually he expanded the poems with so-called *wing words* on the sides.

wroth with twone nathandJoe
A
Malt
jhEm
Shen

pftJshute
sOlid man
that the humptYhillhead of humself
is at the knoCk out
in thE park

In order to increase production and limit his own interference and intention, Cage had poet Jim Rosenberg develop a software called Mesolist, which read through the source text and picked out the words meeting Cage's criteria and produced a list containing these words. Throwing the dice hundreds of times would have taken him too long, so Cage had another software developed: *IC*[9], which simulated *I Ching* throwing-of-the-dice at a rapid rate. Cage's mesostics however, don't fulfil themselves in book form. They are meant to be read out loud and Cage frequently pointed this fact out himself. Often he would perform his soft, whispering, singsong mesostics in an art gallery or concert hall in an informal setting, in front of a little desk, sitting on a piano stool under theatrical chiaroscuro lighting. It was during these readings – which could last for hours – that his mesostic poetry accomplished his idea of a free language: coincidental, indeterminate and full of change, like nature itself.

Today Cage's mesostic poetry is not particularly well known, and in many people's opinion it does not hold the same liberating artistic force as does *4'33"*. In Cage's time poetry as a field was in many ways more explored than music. Many of the paths along which Cage walked in his search for a pure form of poetry were already well trodden by Dadaists, lettrists, futurists and the *Noigrade* group's concrete poetry. In the United States for example, poets such as William Carlos Williams, Charles Ohlson and Jackson Mac Low had written poems featuring coincidences and already existing work. Another factor contributing for the limited impact of Cage's *Lectures*, *Diaries* and mesostics is the inherent conservatism of language, compared to music with its more volatile and abstract power of expression. Even if you turn a word upside down, write it in sixteen different fonts and apply a hundred colours to a verse, you will find yourself within a literary logic which produces meaning and continues traditions, and from which it is almost impossible to escape. Perhaps it was not until the 1960s, when Cage began producing his abstract and minimalist lithographs and watercolour paintings at the

Crown Point Press in San Francisco, that he actually managed to adapt his musical conceptions to a paper surface and create a successful visual equivalent to his compositions.

FROM MYCOLOGY TO UTOPIAN ANARCHISM

Outside of the arts sphere, Cage's poetics was also apparent in two other fields: mycology (the study of mushrooms) and social philosophy. When asked about which profession he would have chosen if he could live all over again, Cage's answer was neither painter nor poet, but botanist. Cage's love for mushrooms came about early in his life, during the Great Depression of the 1930s, when he lived in a cottage in Carmel, California. Waking up to find himself completely penniless, Cage was forced to eat the mushrooms growing around his cottage for several weeks. One day he was poisoned and nearly died, after which point he realized he was left with two options: either stay away from mushrooms altogether or learn everything there is to know about them. Cage went for the latter option. He set about collecting mushroom literature, creating a library that would, upon his death in 1992, grow so extensive that it is now stored in the University of California in Santa Cruz. In the 1950s Cage began teaching a course in Mushroom Identification at the liberal arts school The New School in New York, along with his mycology friends Guy C. Nearing and Lois Long. The course grew popular and led Cage to found the New York Mycology Society[10], which still exists today. His interest in mushrooms would also give Cage economic benefits, as several New

York restaurants would have him as their personal mushroom supplier. In 1958 he went to Italy to participate in the Italian version of Double or Quits in which he would answer questions related to mushrooms. A few days later he went home to New York with the first prize in his suitcase – 6 million liras.

Mycology also featured in Cage's writing and music. With his own humorous take on the cooking book genre, Cage published in 1972 the somewhat abstract mushroom cooking book, *The Mushroom Book*.[11] In it he had drawings and lithographs accompanying the anti-syntactical recipes that would doubtlessly leave the reader salivating for a mushroom stew of red toadstool fried in butter. The recipes and methods of identification were not of particular importance to Cage, just like the points of the anecdotes were unimportant in *Indeterminacy*. Cage's objective was for the text to take on a form that would let the mushroom catch the reader's eye just like it does in nature.

One can easily dismiss Cage's mycology as general trivia, but to Cage the mushroom was a symbol of change and of nature's ways of decomposing and rebuilding: its coincidental growth and spore structures make the mushroom hard to place in a rational system. As Cage put it himself: "The more you know them – about telling, for example, a Spathyema Foetida from a Collybia Platyphylla... the less sure you feel about identifying them."[12]

In the accidental growth pattern of the mushroom Cage found a principle he thought adaptable to human society. Just like the mushroom grows freely, humans should live in freedom, without overarching governance structures. In 1988 Cage published the mesostic poetry collection *anaRchy*[13] which consisted of twenty 50% mesostics based on a source text of thirty anarchistic quotes from people as different as Henry David Thoreau, Emma Goldman, Peter Kropotkin and Mikael Bakunin. Up until his death Cage remained a committed anarchist and his poetics were always intended as not only models to liberate the arts but to liberate man and society: "We have, so to speak, managed to create a musical model for a society that is not at all like the one we actually live in, I would say this model is for a better society."[14] Just like Cage left behind old methods and materials to develop a new music built on the basic elements of sound, silence and time, Western society would have to be deconstructed and rebuilt. Already in 1975, Cage wrote:

> Our political structures no longer fit the circumstances of our lives. Outside the bankrupt cities we live in Megalopolis which has no geographical limits. Wilderness is global park. I dedicate this work to the U.S.A., that it become just another part of the world, no more, no less.[15]

For Cage this did not imply simply alterations of old economic and political structures, but a new start, a new society, the building blocks of which would be diversity, immediacy and uncertainty. When society reached this point humans would fully comprehend how governing systems or ideologies are unnecessary, as man is his own centre in time and space. Man would be liberated and as such, noble. At this point man would enter the anarchistic society, which embraces the complexity and chaos of nature, working with it, not against it, like our current political systems.

John Cage has inspired several generations of composers, conceptual artists and anarcho-syndicalists. Cage's art is not a finished chapter that with hindsight can be categorized and looked upon from a lofty academic distance, rather it continues to show the way to realize the aesthetic potential of everyday life. Very few pieces of art bear direct similarities to the art Cage left behind, presumably due to Cage's artistic appeal to break with traditions and systems in order to create something new. At the same time, few theories of art have been abused to the same extent as Cage's; be it the musician who plays out of tune, only to excuse himself with Cage's concept of coincidence, or the experimental artist carrying a splattering paintbrush in one hand and an electric harp in the other, force-feeding his avant garde intentions to the audience. Cage offered liberation, but only under a regime of deep concentration and discipline. This was not camp or hippie ideology, it was 'permission granted, but not to do whatever you want.'[16] Alongside the liberating force in Cage's art, it also contains deep latent political criticism, a diagnosis of our time, in which traditions and deep-rooted systems control society and the human experience. However, as long as there is silence, says Cage, there is hope. All we need to do is listen to the silence.

THE HAMSTER FROM HAMMERSBORG

That which colloquially became known as *The Hamster From Hammersborg* belongs to one of the more eccentric cases in Norwegian media history. After learning from reliable sources that those involved in the case have passed away, it is high time to come out with the truth.

The hamster in question was in all likelihood an ordinary citizen: a secure public job, engaged in popular culture and newly single after a breakup that led to his move to Hammersborg in the capital.

One night he heard a song seeping up from the flat below. Human or vermin, something had moved in. As the night went on, he noticed that it was not the sound of moving boxes that was permeating up through the floorboards. He lay with his ear against the floor and could swear that it was a song playing on repeat. After biting his pillow for several hours, he threw on his robe and stormed down the stairwell. From a newly installed nameplate on the door beamed: *Milton Nascimento – Tudo Que Você Podia Ser.* The more he knocked on the door, the higher up the volume was turned. The door remained unopened.

He Googled extensively. Milton Nascimento was a famous singer and guitarist, heralded as the voice of the Minas Gerais region in southeastern Brazil. What in god's name was this man doing in an apartment block in Hammersborg? Nascimento debuted with the bands *Evolussamba* and *Sambacana* in the small city of Três Pontas before moving to Belo Horizonte. Here he met the musicians Lô Borges and Beto Guedes, and formed the collective *Clube da Esquina*, which would become the most important anti-cultural expression in Brazil together with the Tropicália movement. He continued typing and jackpot... *Tudo Que Você Podia Ser* was a song from the band's debut album on EMI in 1972. He clicked on a video in which a music critic claimed that the song was one of the strongest compositions within the *Música Popular Brasileira* genre. The tune was much beloved by the population as an expression of joy, trespass and transformation. The music critic raised his chin as he announced that the song was one of the first examples of what one calls *antropofagia*: cultural cannibalism that encourages a shameless blend of styles such as classical, progrock, jazz, samba and musical traditions south of the Sahara. The Hamster found the song on Spotify, and as it played from the stereo now on two different stories, he put the title through Google Translate. His heart stopped a beat as he read on the screen: *All that you could have become*. That's when it dawned on him – it was a song that had moved into the downstairs flat.

The weeks that followed saw a flurry of emails going back and forth. It was clarified that the song had a right to remain as a resident as long as it kept below a certain decibel level. A review showed that some individuals could not hear anything, but the Hamster could discern Nascimento's earthly voice with clarity. He didn't see any other option but to take out a loan. The last thing that the acoustician said before he began laying the insulation was – are you completely certain that you don't want to listen to *that* song?

The first weeks felt like paradise. Of course he still felt irritation at the nameplate, but he slept like a baby. However, one day the Hamster became conscious of the silence with which he had surrounded himself and began to feel a hypnotic emptiness where the song had been. Down below was longing, hope and flesh – in short, the ghosts in the pale pink machine. That night he dreamt of his ex who claimed that you haven't seen shit until you've feasted your eyes on a dessert buffet from the Sunnmøre region. He saw mountains of bulging Kvæfjord cake and could taste the nutmeg from the sweet Tropical Aroma cake. He was suddenly transported back to the July 22nd memorial concert for the mass shooting victims, inside the cathedral it was he who stood on the stage now, and not Karpe Diem, and he sang *Tudo Que Você Podia Ser.* His earthly voice healed the Norwegian population. The next morning he tore apart the wood floor, splintering himself to pieces to get down to the song, he could hardly breathe without it.

And that is how they found him. A local journalist snapped the now-famous photographs of the flat that looked like a hamster cage in which one could see glimpses of a person crawling about on all fours in the rubble. Hence the front page spread which stirred outrage amongst the Norwegian population: *The Hamster From Hammersborg.*

NAZI JAZZ

Among all of Berlin's second hand stores, in which the sundries are piled up against the walls, there is one to which I always pay visit. The owner, Herr Munz, an old east German who invariably dresses in a completely blue suit, laments all of the foreigners who leave his establishment without putting down a single coin. He believes the tourists are only out for relics from the Weimar, Nazi or GDR eras. "What is it with these people? In the one era we punched each other, in the next we gassed each other and in the third we spied on each other." But he isn't quite consistent in his own teachings. Namely, on the wall hangs a rare LP of the jazz band Charlie and his Orchestra, priced at over 500 euros.

The story was leaked around the end of the 1980s. One of Europe's most renowned swing jazz drummers, Fritz Brocksieper (1912—1990) came forward and revealed how he had managed to survive with panache during the years 1940—1945. Because, how does one survive who played the type of music that the governing authorities labelled *Amerikanische Negermusik* and declare as degenerate art? There was only a single solution – to join Joseph Goebbel's jazz orchestra.

If Bauhaus was the design expression of the Weimar Republic, swing jazz and the associated swing kids was its musical expression. One man who understood the value of all-encompassing trends was the propaganda minister, Goebbels. He recognized that the theatre of war was not only carried out on the field, in the air or at sea, but also among the airwaves. Not far from Adolf Hitler Platz in Berlin, known today as Theodor-Heuss Platz, was a building that housed Deutsche Kurzwellensender (DK), the German Shortwave Broadcaster. With the new shortwave transmitters, it was possible to send recordings from Berlin forth throughout the world, and in 1941 the DK broadcast 147 hours weekly of radio programmes in 43 languages. The main programme, which was aired in the USA and England, contained satirical radio dramas in English, counterfactual stories, and – to keep up a high number of listeners – the voices of the allied prisoners of war who were allowed to tell their loved ones that they were doing well.

This is where Charlie and his Orchestra come in. In 1940, the saxophonist and bandleader Lutz Templin was commissioned to put together a house orchestra for DK with the best jazz musicians in Europe. The singer they brought in was named Karl Schwedler, but in order to give it an anglophile ring, the band was dubbed Charlie and his Orchestra. Throughout the war, Schwedler undertook multiple business trips behind enemy lines in Europe to keep up on the jazz hits in the allied countries. Back at home, the orchestra practiced covers of the biggest hits with the texts mildly rewritten to contain Nazi propaganda. Guy Lombardo's classic *You Are Driving Me Crazy (What Did I Do),* for example, a song about the perilous pathways of love, was instead rewritten as a portrayal of Churchill going mad due to the obvious superiority of Germany and Japan. Cole Porter's *Serenade To Your Girlfriend* became an homage to the German pilots who carpet bombed England, while Irving Berlin's showpiece *Let's Go Slumming* was lightly transformed into *Let's Go Bombing*. In which Charlie croons with his milky voice:

> Let's go shelling, where they are dwelling
> Let's shell Churchill's women and children tooooo
> Let's go to it, let's do it, let's bomb neutrals too!
> Let's go bombing, it's becoming, quite the thing to doooo

But starting in 1943, it was suddenly Berlin that was being carpet bombed, and DK's broadcasts vanished from the airwaves.

Paradoxically, the musicians experienced a renaissance after the war was over. Rumours about the jazz orchestra reached the dance-happy American soldiers, who in post-war years became the orchestra's benefactors in exchange for meat, coffee and cigarettes. Fritz became Freddie, and no one ever mentioned Charlie and his Orchestra. Though the band members stubbornly persisted that their choice had been between a certain death or playing Nazi jazz, and that they were only supplied with the music but not with the lyrics in the studio, there's little doubt that the band profited from the war. Charlie and his Orchestra is a leading example of how music and programmes bound to a political agenda often tend toward unmusicality. But even more telling is that it shows Goebbel's early use of mass media and popular culture in order to win the just as important propaganda war, a strategy that has nowadays become common practice among the super powers.

We are already dreading the music of the next world war.

FRIENDS, I'M STILL SINGING

The word quality is starting to wear thin at the elbows. *Renowned, uncompromising, legendary, important* – all these cursed words we use to dig a moat to fend off mediocrity. But that's how inflation happens in a language, and adjectives feel hollow when we, on a rare occasion, encounter a truly exceptional work of art. Just as now, as I listen to Sidsel Endresen's album *So I Write*, and the only thing I can do is to take out a needle and strong thread of enthusiasm to patch up the elbows.

We are living in the days of the CD bonfires. Although the first edition rare CD albums are starting to fetch high prices, I am on my way downstairs to clean out the cellar. Where did Bahamadia, Boogiemonsters, Real Live or The Brotherhood go? Or what happened to the spoken word poet Ursula Rucker? Did the hippie-hip-hoppers Arrested Development fall down a rabbit hole in a field of poppies? Is DJ Krush's *Meiso* still considered an untainted masterpiece? Did I really finance HMV's executive salaries by listening to Rae & Christian, Talvin Singh and Helén Eriksen? And wasn't the horrorcore rappers like Gravediggaz, Flatlinerz and Killarmy ten times more hardcore than any black metal? Odd Børretzen! And what ever happened to Kølla og Bølla, aka Kolbotn Playboys? Buried beneath this human pile of forgotten rap artists from the 90s is my copy of Sidsel Endresen's *So I Write*. Because I no longer have a CD player in the house, I go sit out in my Toyota Corolla parked in Åkerbergveien with the overhead lamp on and push in the disc.

Some voices stick in your skull from the first moment you hear them – Lotte Lenya, MF Doom, Curtis Mayfield or Karen Dalton – you wish to hear more of that particular frequency no matter what it is that comes out between their beaks. Sidsel Endresen has such a vocal cord, and among her back catalogue, the album *So I Write* on ECM in 1990 is one of the highlights. It is here that one finds Endresen interlaced with the musicians Jon Christensen, Django Bates and Nils Petter Molvær, and the quartet takes the listener through eight compositions that feel as though they've sprouted out of an inner necessity. At first, the subdued mood can seem inordinately simple and easy-going, but beneath the surface is a temperament and broodiness that lends the songs a powerful internal tension. The strength to grow inhabits each tune. The poet Endresen also emerges on this album. *Truth* and *Dreamland* are two of the most beautiful song lyrics that I know, it feels painful when she phrases the words. The music cracks open a forgotten inner world, and makes us appreciate our own poetic abundance. These clear, unsentimental moments in which we understand that we are little more than worker ants and primates inching upward along the rope. A knock on the window. My line of thought is broken by a Somalian taxi driver who is on his way to evening prayers in the Tawfiiq Islamic Center and wonders whether I'll be driving out soon.

In 1937 the French surrealist André Breton wrote: "There could be no higher artistic teaching than that of the crystal. The work of art... considered in its deepest meaning, seems to me devoid of value if it does not offer the hardness, the rigidity, the regularity, the lustre on every interior and exterior facet, of the crystal." Sidsel Endresen has stated that she creates a strict framework, replete with traps, and challenges her vocal muscles before going out on stage – creation should be difficult. Each song is comprised of thousands of detailed choices and one should not simply resort to trust formulas or automation. One must be open for the unexpected to happen. Sidsel Endresen is crystal.

Her musical journey has lasted for over 30 years. At a concert during the Oslo Jazz Festival in 2009, a lady yelled at her: "Oh, Sidsel, couldn't you play something from *Jive Talking*?" (Editor note: SE's hit song with Jon Eberson Group from 1981). I thought that Sidsel Endresen was going to walk slowly off of the stage, tear the head off of the lady and put it on a stake as a warning to show all of her *Jive Talking* fans what she thinks about becoming static as an artist. But she let it go. The lady in the audience was only one of thousands of detailed choices that Sidsel had to take in the course of a single concert, and she chose to ignore it.

Bless her efforts.

MUSIQUE BRUTE

One publication that I greatly value is the catalogue from the exhibition *Broken Music – Artists' Recordworks* which was shown at the DAAD Galerie in Berlin in 1988. This contains the works of composers and visual artists who use vinyl records "to alienate, destroy, paste together or simply to use them differently," as it is stated in René Block's introductory text. He highlights Richard Rayner-Canham's photograph of the chanteuse Hermine, who is putting records into the dishwasher, as an example of how some artists and musicians do not view vinyl as a fixed reproductive medium, but rather as a foundation for innovative meaningful sound and visual art. Within the catalogue we find Christian Marclay's grooveless record, Marcel Duchamp's optical discs and Milan Knizak's cracked, glued-together and painted 7" which serve to undermine the records' intended purpose as bearers of sound. Another publication that is included in the beautiful catalogue is the vinyl case *Expériences musicales* containing six 12" with the music of French visual artist, architect and composer Jean Dubuffet (1901—1985).

Dubuffet is considered a central visual artist of his generation and is a standard feature for the collections of modern museums on par with Picasso and Klee. As a young man, he came across the book *Bildnerei der Geisteskranken* (Artistry of the Mentally Ill) by the psychiatrist and art historian Dr. Hans Prinzhorn from 1922. Here, Prinzhorn maintained that the animal instinct and the pure brutality that one could find in the artistic expressions of inpatients and children gives the viewer a spiritual strength that puts him in harmony with the universe. Inspired by Prinzhorn, Dubuffet strived to create art that was primitive, anti-intellectual and violent – an existential expression that everyone might understand. These ideas were first developed in his distinctive paintings in which Dubuffet used organic materials such as sand, tar and straw, combined with an *impasto* technique – paint applied in thick layers on the canvas. He later turned his vision to architecture and music. He named the child – *art brut* – the crude art.

The year 1960 would mark the first outing for Jean Dubuffet's musical works. With encouragement from his bosom buddy, the Danish Cobra-artist Asger Jorn, Dubuffet formed an improvisation collective in his house in Paris. The two visual artists had one thing in common: both were musical imbeciles. Jorn could play a bit on trumpet and violin, while Dubuffet was a happy amateur on the bagpipes and accordion. The next step in the *how-to-make-an-improv-band* learning curve was that Dubuffet went on a shopping spree to the musician and instrument maker Alain Vian's shop in Rue Grégoire-de-Tours. He gathered here several cases of rare instruments from different parts of the world, together with a handful of Vian's home-forged curiosities, and he asked the shop owner to join the band. In this way, Dubuffet and Jorn invited their artist friends and tagalongs, even several random passersby, to partake in their collective concerts. Dubuffet assured his fellow musicians that their lack of musical education was not a problem. The goal was not to display virtuoso techniques but rather to use the instruments to achieve unconventional effects and unusual sounds. The studio manager was none other than Dubuffet himself, who employed a cheap Grundig T35-tape recorder hooked up to a single microphone with which he walked around the room. The fact that the sound quality was extremely lo-fi and shabby was in no way taken as a negative. Just as in his visual art, Dubuffet was out after a raw, organic mode of expression in the sound. He asserted that all of the creative spheres might use earthlier techniques to their advantage in order that art would descend from its intellectual cloud and meet the ordinary. Following the footsteps of the Art Ensemble of Chicago and Otto Muehl's sound orgies in Vienna, Dubuffet's home was crammed full of sound for three months; the house was converted into Serafin's incomparable music machine. The result of these séances was released in the box set *Expériences musicales* by the company Edizione Del Cavallino Venezia in 50 signed copies. The six covers were drawn by Dubuffet himself and were black-white lithographs depicting the wild recording sessions.

Jean Dubuffet's visual art remains a dilemma to this day. He claimed that his artistic oeuvre represented anti-culture, yet the first thing that happened upon his debut in 1944, was that the bourgeoisie wished to have one of "the wild beasts" hanging on its silk covered walls. This certainly did not happen with his music, however. Even though Dubuffet recorded five albums over the course of his career, none of these are now available, except as digital bootlegged versions on UbuWeb.com. His musical output is the ultimate bastard of brutality, fear and idiocy – the impressions are so direct that every well-tempered listener must man his or her barricades of good taste. Dubuffet himself emphasized that the experiments should be taken as sketches of an idea from someone who has taken a first pioneering step into unknown territory.

BEAT BOP

There is a nightmare raging inside of me. The sheets stick to my burning back as I stand up. In order to keep the bed-peace, I once again blame the warmth of the double blanket, but I know, darling, that I've had that nightmare again: I find myself in a courtroom and to the right I can see all of Norway's free jazz, improv and noise-making community gathered in the dock. Between all of those beards, I can see the top of Lasse Marhaug's head, the eyes of Maja Ratkje and the tips of Paal Nilssen-Love's drumsticks. On the other dock to the left, I see half of Norway's art world who are conversing nervously. The buzz of conversation quiets as the judge bangs the gavel and bids silence in the court.

> The verdict has been decided. The noise-making, improvisation and free jazz folks – I sentence you to death for crimes against the environment based on an enormous CO2 footprint from your countless trips around the globe, and for your use of printers in the East where there are no labour laws.

He turns his gaze over to where I am sitting, and declares:

> Art folks – I sentence you to death for having printed up millions of catalogues and anthologies that

no one willingly reads and which no one has ever bought. You shall feel the same pain as the Latvian forests; murdered, cut down, mashed to pulp so you can sit eternally in the cold cellars of institutions!

I wake and I feel that I have no more worth than the sweat in my sheets. After a night like that, I must find an antidote that can prove that all which is resistant, which is obscure, which is avant garde actually has some relevance. I walk over to the milk crate and pull out my Dutch bootleg copy of Rammellzee and K-Rob's 12" *Beat Bop* — the one with the hand-drawn cover produced by visual artist Jean-Michel Basquiat, which costs 1000 euros if you're lucky enough to get an original.

We are not worthless.

The story behind this release is as unique as the sound that is contained in its grooves. The graffiti writer, high priest of Gothic Futurism and rapper Rammellzee (1960—2010) had at times a turbulent relationship with his friend Jean-Michel Basquiat (1960—1988). According to the myth, following an argument, the visual artist wanted to bury the hatchet with a classic rap battle in the studio. When he showed the verses, his opponent laughed, tore the page into bits and kicked Jean-Michel out the door. Together with the rapper K-Rob, he locked himself into the studio and didn't see the light of day until they had committed the epic ten-minute long *Beat Bop* to tape. The duo decided that their *back-and-forth* rapping should take the form of a role play: Rammellzee would be the dope-addicted pimp on the street corner while K-Rob would play the innocent school boy on his way home, with temptation and sin all around. As the needle moves toward the centre, the text moves from simple social realistic observations and rhyme battles to more abstract and indefinite wordplays, nasal voices and delayed responses.

Although Rammellzee later asserted that the only thing Basquiat did was to pay the studio bill, there is little doubt that Basquiat's production and LP cover design has helped to cement its status as a classic. The beat starts in an old-school no man's land between blunt disco, conga-driven funk and 808-drums. But in the middle of the piece, Basquiat turns the whole thing on its head. There is now a prolonged use of echo and reverb on the vocals, distorted improvised violin riffs, and layer upon layer of percussion and other sonic frills performed by the musicians Al Diaz and Eszter Balint. It is therefore not without basis that *Beat Bop* has been called the first psychedelic and avant garde rap song, or hip hop's *Ulysses* for those who prefer a much more powerful patron. It is as though the elements from New York's Downtown scene, from no-wave, disco, minimalism, transgressive cinema and graffiti culture are summed up in one and the same tune. *Beat Bop*'s strength is that despite its twisty-bag-mix, it sounds neither feigned nor spasmodic; it is quite simply a hip-hop banger even today.

If Rammellzee won the battle, he lost the war. Jean-Michel Basquiat got hold of the master tapes from the studio, printed 500 copies and released it with his own record company Tartown Records in 1983. With his unmistakable neo-expressionistic manner, Basquiat drew a cover that was unlike any other posed rap cover at the time. To put the final nail in Rammellzee's coffin, he spelled his name with only one L, something which bothered his rival to his last days, as his name was in fact "a quantum mechanic equation, you don't spell it with one L." But the song would not end up as a mere curiosity. Basquiat sold the master to Profile Records, and when the iconic graffiti film *Style Wars* used *Beat Bop* as the theme song, it sold 150 000 copies. Rammellzee, who had long desired to become a dentist, ended up going for a creative profession.

'YOU SMILE WHEN YOU CRY'

We were members of the well-off working class, or more precisely, west side boys lacking prospects for summer jobs. The teacher said we would have an exam on Snorri Sturluson's sagas, so we adopted the phrase: *Kill me, dear king, but not with porridge!* But we didn't have exams that year, one boy in the B-class died suddenly in a bicycle accident so everyone simply got a pass. After the funeral we cycled down to Skarspsno and hung around Ebbe's bedroom. He snuck into his big brother's room and borrowed an album. We were fifteen years old and discovered house music's prototype – Manuel Göttsching's *E2-E4.*

In these days of audiophiles, in which the preferred listening experience is nearing *white cube* standards, in which kids in the prime of life meet at a club to sit quietly listening to an album together, in which the Øya Festival has a stage rigged by the HI-FI club – it is high time to admit that music is best listened to when dancing, drinking, driving, weeping, running, raging waking, dreaming and in a brawl. Or my personal favourite – when being strangled. Regardless what brand the loudspeakers might be.

Of all the strange things I did in my youth (including sending excrement by post to a paedophile priest and cutting myself in the face with a fish filleting knife in order to win sympathy from a girl), listening to music while being strangled takes the cake. My package was returned in the mail and the girl thought my wound was "disgusting", so the strangling is also, in retrospect, the most rewarding of these activities. This was pre-Internet, so who knows precisely who came up with the idea; maybe one learned it at summer camp from the older boys, maybe someone or other had stayed up late watching cable TV without permission? Ebbe said he was going to show us something wicked, hopped up onto the box spring mattress and stood with his back against the corner. He then began to hyperventilate. Without warning, he positioned the palms of my hands around both sides of his throat, and pressed it in toward the wall. I tried to remove my hands, but he held onto my grasp until his eyes rolled up behind their lids. Ebbe sank down along the wall and onto the mattress. A few seconds later a jolt passed through his body. He smiled sleepily, floundered, said it was soooo good, it felt like he'd been sleeping for ages. "It's not dangerous, does anyone else want to try it out?"

Once Ebbe suggested that we should each have a turn being strangled, it wasn't hard to convince us. As Götsching's irresistible house groove hyped up the mood, we stood in a row and hyperventilated to the beat. Then the executioner would come lay his palms against one's throat, and we went down for the count, one by one. We woke partially layered on top of each other, lethargic, we'd travelled to far off galaxies and were at peace. "More, more – strangle for a little longer! And put the needle back to the beginning!"

And then it was my turn to play executioner. I strangled effectively until a heap of buddies lay piled on the mattress. One by one they returned to consciousness, but Sigurd lay stiffly on the bottom. I shook him, but there was no sign of life. "How long did you strangle him for, actually?" I tickled him, and then pinched the fat in his side, but his body was just as dead. I cried and laughed at once. The others claimed no responsibility. As I prepared to give mouth-to-mouth, an enormous grin grew across his jaw. Sigurd's eyes popped open, he pointed at me and screamed: "You smile when you cry."

Whenever I listen to *E2-E4* today, that hour long cosmic house suit produced by the German guitarist and composer Manuel Göttsching in 1981, I think that it was responsible for arousing our strangle-lust. *E2-E4* tears you away, lifts you up, puts you into a thick trance of happiness – sublime and minimalistic. The earth is a sinful song, and Manuel Göttsching is playing rhythm guitar.

THROW OPEN THE CHURCH'S DOORS!

It took a while for the Norwegian church to ask itself the question: why should the devil have all the good music?[17] Church music has at all times been subject to the Platonic notion that music has an inherent power which can refine and cultivate mankind. A power which can also, through its appeal to the senses, corrupt it.[18] In the Old Testament, in which Jewish traditions are firmly rooted, another point of view is found. In psalm 150 in the Psalms it says: "Praise him with the sound of the trumpet: praise him with the psaltery and harp / Praise him with the timbrel and dance." But with the arrival of the New Testament the church shifted the focus to the Word of God. Music no longer had a value in itself, but merely acted as an instrument for serving and broadcasting the divine Word.[19] It was then that Church music became vocal and ascetic, precipitating the erection of churches with acoustics adapted to the purpose of preventing heathen, drum-banging music being performed in them. And this division between religious and heathen music is one that has been maintained up to modern times.

But with the great transformations within youth and popular culture in the 1960s there also came a renewal within church music. In the course of a few years, the gospel-soul of Sam Cooke and

Aretha Franklin had snuck down from the pulpit to the dance floor, and Duke Ellington's *Sacred Concerts* and John Coltrane's *Love Supreme* drew Jesus into the jazz clubs. And even though the Rolling Stones sympathised with the devil and Robert Plant worshipped Aleister Crowley, Christian communities embraced rock'n'roll as it was, spearheaded by Larry Norman and Love Song.

THE ORIGINAL ROCK'N'ROLL PRIESTS

In the Norwegian film *Broder Gabrielsen* from 1966, Alf Malland plays the lay preacher Gabrielsen who realises that he is going to need more than the Word of God to convert the youth of the day. Cunningly, he discovers that by mixing the Word of God with rock'n'roll, he can reach a point of ecstasy that draws flocks of lambs to his meetings. *Broder Gabrielsen* created a huge debate about the numerous arrivals of lay preachers and hallelujah-evangelism in Norway. On top of this the revivalist preacher and singer-songwriter Aage Samuelsen sued the makers of the film for creating a malevolent portrayal of his life. But for the most part *Broder Gabrielsen* portrayed the change that had taken place in church life in the 1960s, with the welcoming of popular music and a more open liturgy. It is no coincidence that this change took place in the free churches connected to the Pentecostal movement, the Missionary society and the Lutheran Evangelical church. The pioneers of these movements, Gustav Adolph Lammers (1802—1878) and Thomas Ball Barratt (1862—1940) had in their own time been rebelling against the Norwegian national church, and their rock aesthetics could be felt in the churches' walls. In many of the free churches it wasn't just that the ceilings were lower and there was better acoustics, there was a higher acceptance for what could be tolerated within the space of the church. The free churches also practiced a more open form of meeting and liturgy, making it increasingly easier for young musicians to try out their talents there.

If you search through the massive heaps of Norwegian EPs released on the Christian record companies Ansgar, ETON and Klango before 1970, you will find hours of congregation house quartets and choirs. But there are a few honourable exceptions. In many ways Aage Samuelsen could be called Norway's first rock'n'roll priest. Samuelsen travelled around with several jazz and dance bands in the 1930s, and gained an understanding of secular forms of music. However also important is the fact that Samuelsen was the first Christian artist that openly said he had not always walked the straight and narrow and that he had gone down sinful paths. Standing on stage in front of the Maran Ata congregation with a Gretsch guitar in his hands he was practically on the verge of committing rock'n'roll – only the high-hat was missing.

Another early rock'n'roll priest in Norway was the writer of psalms and the general secretary of Kirkens Bymisjon (the Church's City Mission), Olaf Hillestad (1923—1974). In 1963 he was awarded the Theology Department's Hallesby Scholarship to research jazz and rhythm in Norwegian churches, which he did by looking also at the alternative British jazz masses. As a priest working in the cellar church in Slettebakken in Bergen, he continued his effort to hold rhythm services for the youth of 1963. The leading church musicians of the time wrote in letters to Hillestad, after hearing about his services that, "if this is what it takes to get the youth to listen, then we're not interested." In 1967 Hillestad took an important step forward in founding *Forum Experimentale* in Oslo, an organisation that promised in its statutes to: "boldly work for a renewal in service life, church music and church art."[20] Hillestad acquired premises in Bogstadveien 49c in Oslo that quickly became a breeding ground for young, alternative church culture. It served both as a chapel and youth club where young Christians could worship their God with poetry recitals, art, acid rock and theatre. In 1974, the same year as Hillestad died, *Forum Experimentale* became the record company Kirkelig Kulturverksted – KKV – and the first album they released included Olaf Hillestad's psalms and was titled *Lukk opp kirkens dører* (Open Up the Doors of the Church).

That church music was in a progressive phase was proven in 1966, when Arvid Wangberg emerged as Norway's first Christian crossover-pop star with the EP *Jerikoveien* (The Jericho Road) on Philips. The record sold in big numbers and he followed it up with the album *Arvid Wangberg and the Gospel Group* released on Ansgar the next year; it sold 25000 copies. Wangberg became the first Christian artist to get a review in a secular music publication such as *Pop-revyen*, something that caught Arne Bendiksen's eye, someone who would go on to release Wangberg's follow-up album called *Arvid Sings 12 New Songs.*

FROM TEENAGE SINGING TO JESUS REVOLUTION

In 1967 the Teenage Singing revolution came to Norway. Kjell Grønner was hired as a youth priest in the Bergen YMCA in 1965 and quickly reasoned that something had to be done in order to get the youth of Bergen to attend church. Travelling in Germany that year, Grønner got to experience the American Christian show *Up With People!* with the band Sing Out. He invited them to Bergen, and inspired by their visit, he started Norway's first Ten Sing choir in 1967. Ten Sing developed over the following years to become a concept for YMCA/YWCA's work with Christian youths, focusing on music and theatre. The pillars of Ten Sing were youth participation, open admission, equality and solidarity and their motto was CCC – *Culture. Creativity. Christ.* Other pioneers within the movement were Holm Holmsen and Sigurd Oseberg who started the choir *Crossing* at Holmen church in Asker in 1968, and Sindre Eide who founded *Sky Sing* in Stavanger the same year. Finally, young people came to the churches. And since the choirs were run by young people, the sound in turn was equally young. Compared to earlier choir music there were now drums, electric bass, rhythm guitar, horns and hammond organs. The young people integrated the latest trends from the USA and England into their sound, and thoroughly refurbished Norwegian psalms with rock'n'roll, beats, jazz and protest singing. Ten Sing is one of the biggest success stories in Norwegian music history, and has – besides marching bands – been one of the main suppliers of musical talent to Norwegian music.

A few years later the Jesus movement swept over Norway, a Christian 68-revolt that grew strongly during the 1970s. The Jesus movement that existed in the USA was a radical form of Christianity that merged leftist ideas and hippie-ideals with the Bible. LSD and free love were substituted for a liberated enthusiasm for Jesus. The Jesus movement came to Norway via Sweden, which had been visited by the biggest stars of the movement like Jim McInnes and Duane Pederson. They were in turn invited to Norway and this led to the rise of Norwegian fractions like *Ung Visjon* (Young Vision) in Molde and *Jesu Glede* (Jesus' Joy) in Gjøvik.[21] With the collective *Guds Fred* (The Peace of God) – located in Grønland in Oslo – and *Fredens Bolig (In The Home Of Peace)* in Krokskogen, came the strongest manifestations of the Jesus movement in Norway. In their offices in Nordbygata where the Inner Mission ran The Young Social Team for drug-addicted youth, *Guds Fred* held bible studies, community singing classes and poster workshops. The collective became a noticeable part of the city as they produced hundreds of posters and stickers with contemporary design that they posted everywhere. Che Guevara and Zappa typically traded place with Jesus. *Guds Fred* especially made their presence known by being active in the field of music. They wrote "street songs", to be used when they evangelised on the streets of Oslo. When the cardinal of Oslo, Leif Salomonsen, got in touch to initiate a potential cooperation, it resulted in monthly gospel nights in The Church of the Holy Trinity where as many as 2000 people gathered in the pews and down the aisle. The lead characters in the collective were the protest singing quartet Kari Hansa og Gregers Hes, consisting of Kari Saastad, Hans Olav Mørk (Hansa), Gregers Lund and Hans Erik Schei (Hes) who were to release two albums through the Lutheranean Mission's music department. With personal and heartfelt lyrics about life as a descendant of Jesus and a critical stand against Norwegian society's overabundance and consummation, Kari Hansa og Gregers Hes became the best known manifestation of the Jesus movement in Norway. The sound of the band was more progressive than other folk groups, and they collaborated with well-known secular artists like Trond Villa from Folque and Pete Knutsen from Popol Ace.

Arnold Børud represented a lesser radical branch of the Jesus movement in Norway. In 1971 his rock musical *The Ballad of Jesus* hit the Christian community like a bombshell. In the vein of Galt McDermot's *Hair* Børud wrote a musical for Hamar Cathedral's youth choir called *Praising,* a story of Jesus' life that was aired on prime time national television. This success resulted in the youth of Hamar turning up to church for daily prayers at seven in the morning, and in them going to church instead of watching the local football team Ham-Kam play at Briskeby Gressbane. A lot of parents got worried about this, and Børud was eventually fired from his position as choir leader and conductor. He then initiated the inter church youth choir *Tvers* who worked out of Filadelfia in Hamar. *The Ballad of Jesus* became so popular that in January 1974 Børud went into Roger Arnhoff's sound studio to record the musical with *KERYX* and a string of Norway's finest jazz musicians as a backing band, with *Mini-Tvers* on vocal tracks. The raw and compressed jazzrock sound on the album was developed with Håkon Berge and Finn Pedersen, and the record became so popular that Børud re-recorded it in 1984. Børud also joined the super gospel-group *Frisk Luft (mot åndelig forurensning)* (Fresh Air [Against Spiritual Pollution]), and established *Børud-Gjengen* (The Børud Gang) who spread the Jesus revolution to the ordinary Norwegian household.

With Ten Sing and the Jesus movement there was no way to reverse the reformation of Norwegian church music. During the 1970s stars like Andrea Crouch, Edwin Hawkins and Larry Norman were all booked for gigs at Folkets hus (the People's House), and displayed to the young people that God could be praised in all musical genres. The Christian youth started their own bands, put song books together, created distribution networks and travelled in considerable numbers to music festivals like *Tenåringstreff* (Teen Meeting), *Jesusfestivalen* (The Jesus Festival) and *Gospelfestivalen* (The Gospel Festival).

SING A NEW SONG FOR THE LORD!

As this revival spread across Norway, a powerful Christian record industry grew in its wake. The Norwegian Lutheran Inner Missionary Society started the Luther Foundation's Music Department, which was to become one of the biggest Christian record companies in Norway. Even though young Christians considered Lu-Mi to be quite conservative, the label signed allot of the "hottest" Christian bands in Norway under A&R Nils-Tore Andersen. In addition to the previously mentioned releases of Kari Hansa og Gregers Hes and Arnold Børud, they also signed the jazz band That's Why who originated from the circle around *Forum Experimentale.* That's Why consisted of Jan Simonsen, Per Arne Løvold, Kristian Røstad and Gerd-Elin Sørensen, plus additional appearances from several jazz studio musicians in the Roger Arnhoff Studio. Lu-Mi released the group's two albums, and it is on their second album *That's Why* that the band's electric jazz, reminiscent of Marc Moulin and Eddie Henderson and mixed with interpretations of Christian poets like Alfred Hauge, Aslaug Vaa and Oskar Stein Bjørlykke, really shines through. Lu-Mi also produced The Heralds' debut album. A beat, or in their own words "rhythm" group, that came out of Sinsen Church's youth association. Another band in Lu-Mi's ranks was the Ten Sing choir Sky Sing, consisting of a group of youths from Stavanger that totalled 140 musicians, technicians and singers led by the young priest Sindre Eide. The choir was backed by the progressive orchestra KERYX, and released the album *Vis oss veien*! (Show Us the Way!) in 1972, a Norwegian jazz-gospel record that is a rare gem from the period. Another important record in Lu-Mi's catalogue is *Si det som det er* (Tell it Like it Is) performed by Angelos, the Evangelical Lutheran Free Church and Oslo's Western Congregation Choir, led by Sigvald Tveit. The record was a Norwegian edition of the American Christian hit-musical *Tell it Like it Is – A Folk Musical about God* by Kurt Kaiser and Ralph Carmichael. The cover showed photos of longhaired young people leaning on amplifiers and fender-rhodes' with a Mark Boyle/Joan Hills light spectacle in the background – and some of the music sounds just like that.

The Pentecostal church also had their business up and running. On their label Klango, owned by Filadelfiaforlaget AS, they cut some golden records – selling over 20000 copies – with prominent artists like Kjell and Odd and Karsten Ekorness. But to reach the younger generation they started the sub-label JOY in 1971, and the first record they released was with the band Joyful Singers from Kristiansund entitled *Dette er livet* (This is Life), which was heavily influenced by British beat music.

The JOY label followed this release with other contemporary, young, Christian bands like Young Christians and the jazz-rock band Good News, one of the diamonds in the Norwegian Christian catalogue. The band belonged to the Pentecostals in Ålesund, and was led by Finn Pedersen, who at the time was under the musical influence of Blood Sweat and Tears. In August 1972 they went into Roger Arnhoff's studio and cut their first record with prominent school of jazz musicians like Ditlef Eckhoff, Knut Riisnæs and Bjørn Johansen. The exquisite jazz-rock of the album, with overdubbed moogs and Bernard Purdie-inspired drums, is indebted to the deft finger work of Finn Pedersen, who would later go on to become the house producer for both Klango and Lu-Mi and be involved in over 150 productions.

The record company side of Kirkelig Kulturverksted – KKV – (The Churches Cultural Workshop) was to become one of Norway's big Christian music success stories, with the producer and songwriter Erik Hillestad and sound technician Alf Christian Hvidsteen working as central figures. Besides releasing artists like Bjørn Eidsvåg and Sondre Bratland, the KKV were instrumental in blending and fusing elements of rock and jazz into church music. In their catalogue they have for instance numerous jazzed up psalms performed by the Arne Domnèrus Quartet, Iver Kleive and the Ytre Suløens Jazz Ensemble. In the catalogue there's also treasures like the folk group Slips & Vilt, Ryfylke Visegruppe and the impassioned singer-songwriter Rolf Wagle, who in 1975 released the LP *Jeg vet jeg ikke skal dø* (I Know I Am Not Going to Die). KKV also collected audio recordings from *Tenåringstreff 76* in Sandefjord on the release of *Alt er ditt festivalen 76`* (Everything is Yours Festival). Among those recordings one can find both Bjørn Eidsvåg's debut on record and KERYX comeback performance with a new line-up doing a version of Cedar Walton's *The Loner.*

The secular record industry soon realised the financial opportunities in the crossover-potential of Christian artists. Arne Bendiksen soon signed KERYX, who released their first and only album *Underveis* (On Our Way) on his label. On his sub-label – Forum – Bendiksen released Crossing's ambitious third album *Lyset* (The Light) in 1972. This was an album too experimental for the Lu-Mi label who had released Crossings first two albums, so Hillestad contacted Bendiksen. In addition to the established industry there were many Christian groups who started their own independent record companies in order to release their own records. For example a group of friends from different free churches were the force behind the company Power Music. This consisted of, among others, Styrk Jansen, Per Arne Øienstad and Rune Bratfoss. Under the leadership of Jansen they decided to produce and release a certain brand of jazz-rock and pop, represented by bands like Soli Deo and Presens. As Styrk Jansen worked with video production, he made and directed music videos for all nine songs on Presens' debut *Søker svar* (Looking for Answers). Not bad for an album that ultimately sold around a thousand copies. Soli Deo were also the backing band for Larry Norman when he played in Norway. Allot of the same people from Power Music were involved on the debut album *Kallet* (The Calling) from the now famous gospel-choir Reflex, released on the independent label Miriam Produksjoner. Another nugget in the private pressings catalogue is Grete Salomonsen's debut from 1970. Salomonsen was a folk singer from Kristiansand, connected to the Lutheran Free Church, and was strongly inspired by Judy Collins. She would later release a split-LP with the band Sjeminit! on Lu-Mi in 1972, but in 1970 she was assigned to produce an EP from which the revenues where to go to the Radio mission that operated from behind the Iron Curtain. She gathered a gang of local musicians, with Bjørn Vige in front, and recorded this rare EP.

FROM FORUM EXPERIMENTALE TO SUB CHURCH

The Jesus-revival that swept across Norway in the 1970s diminished in force by the beginning of the next decade. As is often the case with revival movements they come along with a bang at first, only to slowly ebb away over the years. But during that decade Norwegian church music had been shaken to the very core, and a new Norwegian song and psalm-catalogue was created. And plenty of music in this catalogue has survived the test of time well. Had they not been labelled with the prefix "Christian", bands like KERYX, That's Why, Good News and Crossing would surely have contributed with important albums to the general history of Norwegian jazz and rock. Had the radical Jesus imagery been replaced with more digestible leftist imagery, Kari Hansa og Gregers Hes and Aage Samuelsen would surely be an incorporated part of the Norwegian folk movement. The divide between Christian and secular music dissolved in the 1980s when Christian music made its way into the secular music industry. Former Christian artists like Bjørn Eidsvåg, Sissel Kyrkjebø and Sondre Bratland evolved unnoticeably into becoming secular pop stars. And progressive Christian music also picked up pace. Jan Simonsen from That's Why joined prog-rockers Ruphus and Geir Holmsen from Crossings joined the Jon Eberson Group as bass player. Håkon Berge, musical director for many years in KERYX, established himself as one of Norway's most renowned contemporary composers, and is today the director of the Kristiansand Symphony Orchestra. The progressive movement within Christian music passed into the culture surrounding the drug and alcohol free venue Sub Church towards the end of the 1990s in Oslo, which fostered punk rock and shoegazer-bands like Silver, Lionheart Brothers and Serena Maneesh. In the new generation of jazz musicians that blossomed at the same time, a remarkable lot of them had taken their first steps in a Ten Sing choir or learnt how to play the drums in a Pentecostal church. The great modernisation of Norwegian church music in the 1970s wished to *open up the doors of the church*, and one could argue that these doors today have been kicked wide open, albeit more in one congregation than another. The embracing of rock, soul and jazz by Christian music makes sense when you consider the similarity between popular music and the church itself. Both promise their audiences a sense of belonging and salvation. Follow me and devote yourself to me and I will set you free. We are all on our way to Jerusalem.

CAPTAIN NEMO'S EXTRA SUBMARINE

This text unfortunately is not about the Sølvberget Music Library in Stavanger and its place as one of the best in Europe. On the contrary, it is about the over 15 000 albums that no one wishes to acknowledge or to write into musical history. There are no press releases. There's not a single album review or note to be uncovered. No fan has ever gone to any concert with the artists. In fact, there's no one who knows the musicians' names. Welcome to the great world of library music.

My knowledge of this hidden music library began at one of Oslo's now shut down antique shops when I found 47 different LPs with identical covers, all of them moss green with a white frame. The only sign of life was at the top right corner where the letters KPM were written in white, with the anonymous subtitle *Music Recorded Library*. A look at the back showed me album titles such as *Industry vol. 3, Progress And Prestige, The Big Beat* and *Gathering Crowds*. I could not find a trace of artists' names, but beneath each song title there was a descriptive sentence: *Monumental opening of new office building or shopping mall. Street riot beyond limits of control.* Or my favourite: *Shark attack on reggae party.*

I didn't know then that I was holding my first copy of library music in my hands, a stock-photo-archive or a seed bank, if you will, for music. Since the

1960s until today, record companies such as KPM, Music De Wolfe, Peer International, L' Illustration Musicale, Montparnasse 2000 and Selected Sound have produced thousands of albums to set the tone for every imaginable situation, every temperament and every movement within the cosmos. Within this endless library one can find background music so soulless that it would be more spiritual to listen to a real estate agent tattooing Karl Pilkington quotes on the spine of your firstborn. Yet in its stacks one can also find some of the world's most lasting productions within jazz, exotica, electronic music, and kraut. Monty Python, Evergood Coffee and Jay-Z have used their library cards to borrow from this collection.

Although much of the library music is recorded under pseudonyms, today one knows that from well known musicians like Jean Michel Jarre, Dusto Goykovich, Ennio Morricone, Ron Geesin and Manu Dibango, to Norwegian names such as Ketil Bjørnstad, Sigmund Groven, Titanic and Frode Thingnæs recorded library music when times were lean. One unknown name on this list is the Norwegian composer, producer and director Sven Libæk (1938—). Libæk's career started when he landed a role in the international film *Windjammer* in 1958, where he played a singing deck hand on the three-masted full rigger "Christian Radich" together with Harald Tusberg and Lasse Kolstad. The trio formed the band *The Windjammers* and started off on a world tour that brought Libæk to New York and his ensuing studies at the Julliard School of Music. At the start of the 1960s, Libæk moved to Sydney, where he had been offered the prestigious position as A&R for the newly founded CBS Australia. From here, he produced over 200 works with Australian artists in the widening beat- and jazz spheres. In 1968 he began working as a freelance composer and arranger, commuting between Sydney, New York and Los Angeles, where he worked for Lionel Richie, Neil Diamond and the production company Hanna-Barbera. If you've ever seen an episode of Scooby-Doo or The Flintstones, it's likely you've heard some of Libæk's tunes.

It was during his freelance period that Libæk recorded his library music albums *My Thing* with Southern (1970), and *Solar Flares* with Peer International (1974). With titles such as *No Flowers on Venus, Misty Canyon* and *In Nebular Orbit,* it is not surprising that the music should remind one of Martin Denny and Les Baxter's scantily clad exotica, while other songs tend toward the styles of fusion legends like Ralph Lundsten and Marc Moulin. Whenever I listen, it's like dipping into a lukewarm lagoon, losing your sense of direction, sinking further down into the depths and finding there an orchestra of sea anemones, polyps and plankton who are plunking out Libæk's music behind the most stunning coral reefs.

In 2004, Libæk had an unexpected comeback when director Wes Anderson used several of his compositions in his film *The Life Aquatic with Steve Zissou.* The following year, the duo Dangermouse and MF Doom sampled his song *Misty Canyon* on their *DangerDoom* album, and since then Libæk's catalogue has seen a landslide of reissues. Sven Libæk is part of a long line of resurrected heroes like Rodriguez, Bill Fay and Linda Perhacs, who are written into the canon that had originally excluded them, by new generations of music history revisionists. And who isn't touched when David Axelrod is woken in his camper by the postman delivering a check for 1.5 million dollars from Dr. Dre for his use of the former's song *The Edge* from 1967?

When I was tasked several years ago with putting together a compilation of obscure Norwegian music for Tuba Records, Libæk tipped me off that he had been involved in the sound production of an elusive Norwegian film from the 1970s. I don't remember the title and was never able to uncover the audio tapes amongst the archives, but I did come across a folder of stills from the shoots, which I still have. On one photo there's a naked girl standing in a shop window of the fish store at Solli Square in Oslo, where a bar called Champagneria is located today. Above her head is a sign that reads: FISH & GAME and LOBSTER, and she is gaping out at the passers-by in terror.

And I don't miss the fish store at Solli Square. It isn't out of nostalgia that I play Libæk's records on a Tandberg Sølvsuper sound system, but the girl's gaze reminds me that history is always with us, it's just we who forget and repress it. If we could crack open our world of imagination, we would be free to move throughout history, to have access to whoever we wish, from all eras and worlds. If we were able to picture ourselves as parts of a larger tradition, we could go layer by layer down through history together with poets and composers. Down there, in that world, we would be on a first name basis with everyone.

By the way, Dante and Arne say hello.

DRONEJOIK

We had a rented car and three days at our disposal to experience a county the size of Jamaica and the Netherlands together. We drove a hundred and fifty from fishing village to fishing village, swept passed reindeer after reindeer and slept in the backseat with our jeans over our eyes to keep out the midnight sun. But what I remember the most clearly from our trip to Norway's northernmost county Finnmark, are three specific sound experiences.

The first occurred when we pulled over to a rest stop. We could hear Astor Piazzollas *nuevo tango* streaming from an old barn not far away, and despite the unbearable stench wafting toward us, we walked closer. Around the corner, a young man stood shovelling a mass of guts with a metal rake. When he saw us, he turned down the radio, removed his protective mask and explained that poachers had used the barn as their slaughterhouse and left behind "everything extra". He started to rake again, and Piazzolla once again became the soundtrack for sloshing heaps of tainted flesh.

We had our second experience after paying an ungodly fee to enter North Cape. Eager summer workers met us selling mini bottles of North Cape champagne for 20 euros – an old tradition which must be maintained, you know – it therefore wasn't so strange that even the centre felt like a drunken alpine hotel. There was a dance band scene here, 3D cinema, *Children of the Earth* monuments and trolls, and just when things couldn't get any worse, I stumbled upon St. John's chapel. The chapel, designed by the Kirkelig Kulturverksted (The Church Cultural Workshop), is one of the most kitschy art projects of the 1990s, and proof of the church's continued occupation of Lapland. A boat hull alter fits into a groove blasted out of the mountain while a soft blueish overhead light oozes out over the pine furniture, mosaics and textiles procured from some scientology film. And then, as if to shake us up completely, a location-specific composition by Jan Garbarek streamed out from the speakers. I would have liked to read the wording on that project application.

The third sound experience took place on our visit to a lighthouse just outside of Honningsvåg. When one is traveling through northern Norway, there's nothing particularly beneficial about having an eastern Norwegian dialect, for on our way up I was privy to hearing for the umpteenth time how much "Finnmark is being ruined by southerners with suitcases". Inside the lighthouse, I observed stones and shells spread out in formations around the floors and ledges. The guide, who now stood before us as a shaman, explained that spiritualists from all over the world came here to chase away evil spirits that lingered following the Second World War. Far upland we could still see a promontory with remnants of a fort from the war. A rusty tank that no one had bothered to dispose of stood like a prominent scar on the landscape. Once the shaman understood that I worked in music, she presented me with a CD-R on which the words *Beaivi, Áhcážan* had been written.

Even though he is known as the film composer for *Pathfinder* (Veiviseren), and for chanting at the opening of the Lillehammer Olympics, Nils-Aslak Valkeapää, aka Àillohaš (1943—2001) published ten poetry collections and was a visual artist, sculptor and photographer. In addition, he managed to record 17 albums. In his rich discography, there are two releases that stand out: *Goase Dusse* (The Bird Symphony) from 1994 is a principle work in the history of Norwegian field recordings. On this album, Àillohaš brought recording equipment with him up onto the bird cliffs and mixed the uptakes together into a symphony in his studio. The sound is so clear that the listener is able to distinguish the beating wings of birds flapping overhead and diving straight down into the water.

The album *Beaivi, Áhcážan* (To The Sun, My Father) from 1992 tattoos itself on your inside at first listen. With his composition *Divtatt 7-42*, Àillohaš commits dronejoik, to tape for the first time. It starts out calmly, a wall of minimalistic droning that builds up into loops of joiking, chanting, percussion and synthesizers. On top of this, Valkeapää lays down his spoken word. It puts me in mind of Tibetan *pujas* (prayers), classical Indian music and the noise rockers Sunn O))) - but it is the unmistakable sound of Lapland's landscape and vitality. Àillohaš believed in an indigenous universalism in art, and attempted to bring a lost spirituality back to a colonized and Christianized population. My recommendation: push the Nordkapp Centre into the Barents Sea and raise an Àillohaš centre in its stead.

BLOOD IS THE BEST SAUCE

In a memorable scene many years ago, the author Stig Sæterbakken railed on about how the Norwegian translator of Per Olov Enquist's book *Nedstörtad ängel* had committed an error of almost biblical proportions. The book's Norwegian title, *Styrtet engel* (Fallen Angel) implies an angel who has plunged down, more or less by its own fault, and has collided with the earth's surface and all its joys full force. A *nedstörtad* (downfallen) angel, by contrast, has broken through the earth's crust and gone even further down, with all of the symbology which that implies.

During the Christmas season, I watched Edith Jud's documentary about the Swiss artist Dieter Roth (1930—1998), and started to think that *Fallen Angel* would in fact have been a fitting title. Throughout the film's 115 minutes, we follow Roth from the day he arrives at Reykjavik harbour in 1957 with his life packed into two bags. He starts a family with the art therapist Sigrídur Björnsdóttir and produces children's furniture, kinetic art and abstract paintings that are exhibited at the Köpcke Galleri in Copenhagen as well as the benchmark exhibit *Rörelse i konsten* (Movement In Art) at the Moderna Museet in Stockholm. But all throughout the 1960s it's as if a dark and obsessive undertone spreads throughout modernism's utopian and progressive reasoning. *Let there be light!* is exchanged for *Let there be pitch darkness!* At the same pace in which his corporeal volume and alcohol intake double, Roth's artistry balloons outward in a sweat-inducing production of artist books together with Hanns Sohm and Hansjörg Mayer and graphical prints made in collaboration with Richard Hamilton and Arnulf Rainer. He realises megalomaniac projects like the forty-meter long installation *Gartenskulptor* and *Soloszenen*, where Roth painstakingly filmed his attempts at temperance which resulted in 131 VHS cassettes over the course of two years. His Icelandic family has long since been exchanged for affairs financed by taking his paintings underarm to the gallerist Kurt Kalb, who bought the paintings for a sum that would turn Roth into a big spender in Vienna's Yugoslavian restaurants and bordellos for one night.

A little known side to Dieter Roth's artistry is his lifelong relationship with music, as an amateur performance musician, sound artist, label boss and patron. In 1973, Roth started the band *Selten Gehört Musik* (Rarely Heard Music) with Gerhard Rühm and Oswald Wiener, an experimental improv jazz trio somewhere between the Albert Ayler and Harry Partch traditions. And if you think you've ever heard conceptual noise, take another listen to the sound piece *Tibidabo – 24 Stunden Hundegebell* (Tibidabo – 24 Hours of Dog Barking) from 1977, which is comprised of 24 hours of marrow-sucking dog howls, recorded outside a kennel in Barcelona. The following year, Dieter Roth produced *Die Radio-Sonate*, a 45 minute piano and song improvisation for solo performers, moulded by a continuously rising blood alcohol level due to the intake of schnapps after schnapps which resulted in chatting with sound technicians, undesired bodily noises and German tactlessness.

Toward the end of Jud's documentary, Roth's passion for music emerges. You can see the devil in him when he decides to arrange a concert with his big idol Hermann Nitsch – one of the leading members of the loose collective of Viennese Actionism who employed rituals, blood and entrails as artistic materials at whatever cost. Suddenly Dieter appears to be like a stubborn schoolboy trying to get his favourite band to visit his local youth club. Roth hires musicians, rents locales, prints up posters and sells his own artwork to pay for the feast. On October 23, 1980, Hermann Nitsch performs his *5. Sinfonie,* written for forty amateur musicians, at the music academy in Basel. In attendance in the auditorium are fifty audience members who, after a few minutes are reduced to Roth and a few other listeners. In a photograph, one sees Roth in the first row, grinning and captivated by Nitsch's crude symphony from the depths of hell.

Birds of a feather.

BJØRN FONGAARD – A COSMIC COMPOSER WITH A MICRO INTERVALLIC GUITAR

Bjørn Halsten Fongaard (1919—1980), son of Paul Anton Fongaard and Sigrid Hjelmberg, grew up in a working class home in Ekeberg, Oslo. As a child Fongaard built a toy guitar out of a cigar box, and what began as a toy was to become his main instrument throughout his lifetime. Fongaard completed his guitar and piano exams at the Music Conservatory in Oslo in 1945, followed by an exam in orchestra conducting in 1947. Ever since his youth Fongaard viewed composing as his main activity and wrote that "the act of composing comes out of a need to do so, considering it being a natural need in itself..."[22] Fongaard attended private studies in composition taught by Per Steenberg, Karl Andersen, Sigurd Islandsmoen and Bjarne Brustad, though he also took a serious interest in other scientific subjects. Already in 1948 Fongaard wrote: "I can listen to the music within me, but I cannot write it as I do not know the theoretical laws which the music is built upon. That is why I am currently studying physics, chemistry and mathematics more eagerly than ever."[23] Fongaard began intense, autodidactic studies in subjects such as astrophysics, anatomy, chemistry, religion, mathematics, physics, paleontology and a diverse range of languages. Even though he studied on his own, he remained close to both Norwegian and international specialists within the different fields via correspondence, privately initiated meetings and traveling extensively. His studies are reflected in compositions such as *Space Concerto, Uran 235, Homo Sapiens* and *Skapelsen - Orafonia Geo-Paleontoligica*, where he incorporated a narrator reading biblical and scientific texts. His endeavour to become a 'renaissance man' stemmed from the fact that Fongaard saw himself as a composer who worked within humanistic tradition that was several thousand years old. The intention behind his musical expression was to address the fundamental issues encountered in the common human condition:

> I always view music in relation to something, triggered by our surroundings. I view the compilation of basic humanity and the cosmic infinity as the image of total belonging, the order of nature which in its perfection must be the basis of all almighty creativeness.[24]

A MANY-SIDED MAN

Bjørn Fongaard married Bertha Ellinor Johansen in 1950 and they had six children together. To be able to afford and have time for both family life and composing, it was important to keep a neat and systematic way of life. In response to queries as to whether he would keep regular hours when composing or more bohemian ones, Fongaard replied:

> I guess I am quite traditional in that sense. An organized living schedule is an important condition

> that enables me to continue both work and family life. I have a wife and a family of six children demanding my time, which does not leave much time for nonsense. I prefer composing in the morning before the traffic noise is too loud, and we have a cabin by lake Farris where I can retreat to during stressful times.[25]

It is no coincidence that Fongaard was often asked how he found time to manage everything. A closer look at Bjørn Fongaard's work easily leaves one believing he had several doppelgangers. The *studio guitarist* Fongaard participated in hundreds of TV, radio and record productions as a guitarist for Alf Prøysen, Kåre Siem, Vidar Sandbeck, the Bjørklund sisters and the Christian singer Adolf Fjallsett. Throughout the 1960s Fongaard appeared as a regular guitarist on the NRK children's programme *Barnetimen for de minste* and *I kosekroken.*

With his Gibson guitar, the *concert soloist* Fongaard performed alongside the NRK broadcasting orchestra, playing his own variations of themes by Ferdinando Carulli and Niccolò Paganini. The *pedagogue* Fongaard had a regular position as a guitar teacher at the Music Academy (1945—1949), and at the Norwegian Music college (1973—1976), where he also guest lectured in composing. He published two guitar textbooks titled *Med gitaren i kosekroken* (1967) and *Elementær gitarskole* (1972). The *theatre-musician* Fongaard accompanied several theatre performances in Oslo, sometimes even more than one during the same evening. The *jazz and dance musician* Fongaard participated in a jazz band at Kampen in Oslo, led by the American trumpeter Jacques Butler, and even played his way on the ferry from Oslo to New York. If we dig even deeper we discover yet another side to Fongaard's work. He was frequently hired as a *radio and TV-play musician* for pieces by Ingmar Bergman and Anton Tsjechov and the *organist* Fongaard performed both as a church organist and at home playing Bach.

On the other side, Bjørn Fongaard was very much a *composer*. His list of works is unique in Norwegian music history, and he is the biggest composer considering the vast number of works he created. Fongaard's list of works consists of 25 A4 pages of over 150 opus numbers and over 250 composed pieces. His production includes instrumental music composed for symphony orchestras and chamber music, solo pieces made for almost every orchestra instrument, pieces composed for tape recordings and different instruments, and a long list of electronic music composed to be played on the micro intervallic guitar. Fongaard also created music for the ballet: *Relieff* (1968), *Andromeda* (1971) and *Dimensjoner* (1973), and he won the competition for the new evening news jingle with his composition titled *Vignett (Panorama)* in the mid-70s. Fongaard explained that his enormous production was accomplished from keeping to a rapid but in depth working method, inspired by his past as a musician creating music for theatre, often at a very fast speed. Again, when asked the quintessential Fongaard question 'do you consider yourself a very busy man', he replied:

> Busy? Busy – me? No, it all runs by itself, hand in hand. I once went through a period of not compos-

> ing any music for three years and all of a sudden the result of my research into other subjects resulted in pieces of music.[26]

TOWARDS MICRO TONALITY

Even though Fongaard realised his music was seen as *advanced* and *modern*, he never saw himself as independent from tradition.

> Of course I am concerned with renewing myself and my music, though it is important for me to continue building upon the given tradition, not to loose touch with it. I do not try to work against the laws of nature, working with tones and series of overtones given to us by nature.[27]

Fongaard was first influenced by classical modernists such as Hindemith, Schönberg and Webern, and composed works covering most genres, until he began working more in the direction of microtonal systems in the 1960s.

> ...the reason being that I began questioning the existing tonality concept in music. The same way major-, - minor- and church tone structures have their specific recognizable attributes, I believe that the 351 tonal sequences or scales, developed from a 12-tonal system, all have a tonal identity...The purpose with all of this was to show that we have not yet completed our investigation into tonality, at a time when the atonal twelve tone music dominated the development.[28]

In the 1960s Fongaard began composing microtonal works based on tonal systems built upon smaller intervals than half tones, so-called micro intervals. In the beginning, Fongaard used quarter tones made by dividing the octave into 24 equal parts, instead of 12 parts, which is common in tonal music. Fongaard continued researching systems dividing the octave into any possible number. He called these *N-tonal universes,* used to construct new tonal systems. Through dividing the octave he created a series of scales fundamental to his microtonal compositions. Fongaard not only worked with micro tonality in music, he also published three influential manuscripts based around this theme: *Det musikalske selektivprinsipp og 12-tone-universets naturlige høysfæriske tonalitet* (1963), *24-toneuniversets tonale egenskaper og dermed forbundne musikalske muligheter* (1965) and *N-toneuniverset og dets egenskaper som musikalsk byggemateriale* (1967). These detailed manuscripts, based on Fongaard's idealistic and independent research, have made him a European pioneer in microtonal composition today.

One reoccurring problem composing microtonal music in the 1960s was the fact that symphony orchestras were not used to performing such works at the time. Contemporary musicians back then were not used to playing quarter tones, which Fongaard's pieces consisted of, and even though he had been working as a technical drawer for Oslo Lysverker, the musicians were not able to read his accurate graphic notations. This lead to the extraordinary situation where Fongaard work *Uran 235* was delisted from the Oslo Philharmonic Society Orchestra concert in 1965 when the musicians were not able to rehearse it. But Fongaard had another doppelganger up his sleeve. He measured and drew up a model for the instrument he named the micro intervallic guitar, an electric guitar with 24 frets instead of 12. He sent the drawings to a guitar maker who modified a regular 12 fret Framus electric guitar into a 24-fretted guitar, which Fongaard then attached to a simple Maestro guitar amplifier. The 24 different frets on the guitar were painted in different colours to be able to tell them apart. Fongaard himself commented on the micro intervallic guitar and its significance in the NRK TV programme *Composer with a Guitar* in 1971:

> I was searching for an expression for a type of music I felt I theoretically had created already in the 1960s. Back then I had a guitar made with 24 frets instead of 12, a so- called quarter tone guitar. This made it easy for me to work with 24-tone scales, both harmonically and melodically. Having accomplished this I continued researching the musical possibilities working with intervals smaller than a quarter of a tone, towards infinitely small intervals, making very interesting discoveries. This certainly sounds foreign to us, though many other nationalities have used this type of tonal material in their own music since ancient times, in Arabia, India and Bali. The scales were certainly not the only aspect of interest...It was a possibility for me to expand the musical tonality to achieve a more universal expression to a musical feeling.[29]

ELEKTROFONI

Even though Fongaard's guitar was an electronic model, and he used recorders to tape the music and to change the speed, he did not consider his music to be electronic in a common sense. Compared to well known electronic composers, Fongaard never cut the tape, or processed and manipulated sounds through electronic effect boxes or synthesizers. On the other hand, he created unique sounds instrumentally by playing on the micro intervallic guitar, with or without preparations. Fongaard placed pieces of felt, plastic straws and other preparations under the guitar strings. He also had several mutated tuning forks made which he then attached to the neck of the guitar and played the guitar with a specially constructed bow. Fongaard never played the micro intervallic guitar in a normal position: he always placed the guitar on a table that he sat alongside of to play. In Fongaard's universe the guitar has gone from being a normal stringed instrument to become a separate studio where he could design and paint up all sorts of sounds.

Recent documentation shows that Fongaard had a lot of knowledge about electronic music and its possibilities. He went on study trips to electronic studios, Elektronmusik-studion in Stockholm among others, and his notes tell us that he also worked with EMS synthesizers. In 1967 Fongaard made an application to Kulturfondet (the Cultural Fund), asking for funding to build the first electronic music studio in Norway. The application was denied, though in 1972 Fongaard's idea was realized at the Henie Onstad Kunstsenter when NSEM (Norwegian Studio for Electronic Music), was opened.

According to sound technicians, Fongaard often stopped by to record his music for the micro intervallic guitar and to make concert tapes for other musicians performing his music. Fongaard was also involved in the electronic concert series *Elektrofoni* performed at the art centre. Electronic works by Norwegian and international composers were also performed there. Pieces by Arne Nordheim, Karlheinz Stockhausen, Sigurd Berge, Pierre Schaeffer, Kåre Kolberg and Fongaard himself were played from tape in front of a listening audience, a common form of presenting concerts at the time.

In a side note, Fongaard wrote something that looks like a motto for electronic music: "The electronic and new twang varieties... below the human and artistic control of emotions." [30]

NOTHING LESS THAN COSMIC

Fongaard's pioneering within microtonal music and unique exploration of the guitar have made him a cult figure in experimental music. The noise musician Lasse Marhaug describes Fongaard as a "...pioneer in Norwegian experimental music. He was far ahead of his time." The sound artist and producer Helge Sten aka Deatprod, says that Fongaard "...composed some of the most fantastic and captivating music in Norway in modern times. His music is no less than cosmic". Well known Norwegian composers, such as Terje Rypdal, Lasse Thoresen and Egil Kapstad, were all inspired by Fongaard, and recently several music festivals, concert series, and younger musicians have performed his compositions. Some guitarists have even had their own version of the micro intervallic guitar constructed. Even though Fongaard only got to experience a fifth of his work performed during his life time, and never produced a whole LP in his own name, he was (in contrast to the myth surrounding him) a popular composer during his life time. He won several international competitions and was commissioned to compose several large pieces, both nationally and internationally. Fongaard also had his pieces performed by influential musicians at the time, such as Elisabeth Klein, Einar Steen Nøkleberg, Åge Kvalbein, Frøydis Ree Wekre, Brynjar Hoff and Elisabeth Sønstevold, and he received the State Artist Scholarship until the end of his life.

Bjørn Fongaard's work with microtonal music and experimental guitar techniques was 50 years ahead of its time. Today, his guitar tricks and tone systems have become part of contemporary music. The protagonist himself had realized that the cliché about being ahead of the time, was true in his case. But he retained a strong belief that the future people would understand his pioneering work. In a random note, found in his private archive in Larvik, Fongaard wrote: "If I don't succeed this time, it's only for the barricades to fall before the next storm."[31]

'HUSH NOW, HUSH, AND THE LOVELIEST SOUND WILL ARISE'

In the Skillebekk neighbourhood of Oslo – right in the middle where the Dag Solstad character Professor Andersen witnessed a murder and where the Orderud couple were victims of an attempted murder – is an apartment block that houses a ghost. After being fired from my job as a poster hanger for Galleri K, when an owner of a dumpster complained that the gallery posters were regularly tossed there, I got hired as delivery boy at the Brødrene Gondal supermarkct. One of my regular deliveries was to an older gentleman. Within the circumference of his 200 square metre flat he had only room for a bed and a desk with a chair. The rest of the area was occupied by cardboard boxes, and on every single one of these was written: *knick knacks*. Above the chair was a poster for *Vi Kan!* (We Can!) – the craft and industry trade fair that was held at the Oslo harbour in 1938. A propeller plane is hurtling above the trade fair's mascot, Arne Korsmos' 30-metre high spiked-pillar, blasting out "Buy Norwegian, when Norwegian is best!" Atop the desk was the flat's second eye-catcher, a Tandberg Huldra 8 Radio that was always turned on. Occasionally the old man would interrupt me, squeeze his eyes shut, lean his head up next to the speaker and repeat the phrase: "Hush, now hush, and the loveliest sound will arise."

At the same time that civil engineer Vebjørn Tandberg opened his radio factory in 1933, NRK (The Norwegian National Broadcasting Service) undertook a large-scale development of its broadcasting network. No one could yell "Vi Kan!" louder than Tandberg, but Norway's newest industrial mogul came across as a bumbling Mr. Bean with his humble lifestyle and aversion to stimulants in any form. He claimed he lacked talent, but that a handicap in general was a good basis for achieving success. "I was enthusiastic, therefore I succeeded," was his explanation.

Vebjørn Tandberg was much more than only enthusiastic. He implemented his vision of an experimental company that owned itself, and whose employees received welfare benefits that were fifty years ahead of their time. This familial concept drew Norway's best engineers and designers, and in 1951 the company had grown so much that they built a factory in Kjelsås that was 9600 square metres large. In 1962, the factory was expanded with a high-rise that housed a research facility. As the crowning castle, he built the flamboyant Villa Tandberg, which was intended as a place for the "family" to gather. At the boss's insistence, all of the parties ended with a collective jig around the edge of the swimming pool.

Forty years later, the recession came. Under pressure from the Department of Industry, Tandberg was merged with its competitor, Radionette in 1972; the debt of the latter pulled Tandberg down the drain. At the same time, the market was flooded with cheap wares from Germany and Japan. Tandberg, who insisted on quality and solid woodwork, lost major market shares. In 1974, Vebjørn Tandberg retired. However, he still walked to the factory every morning to talk to the workers on the floor. While others could retreat to their wives and children, the factory had been Tandberg's only family. In 1976 and 1977, the factory was so hard up that the state had to take over in 1978. On August 30, 1978, Tandberg received a letter from the factory directors requesting that he discontinue his frequent visits, and informing him that the entertainment venue – Villa Tandberg – where he lived was to be sold. Vebjørn Tandberg sat in his garage, closed the door behind him and turned on the motor.

I have taken my girlfriend out on a sightseeing tour of ruins – a perfect date for a Friday evening. After getting lost between rows of townhouses, we soon find a street named Radioveien (Radio Ave.) When it crosses Lytterveien (Listener Ave.), we know that we are getting close. We round the curve and the old Tandberg Radio Factory appears ahead of us. We recognize the halls of workshops from old photos, even if they are now occupied by fitness studios, calling centres and flats. After a spontaneous photo shoot we get back in the car and drive toward Villa Tandberg. At the corner of Nordbergveien and Krokusveien we catch a glimpse of the old temple's backside. We enter the garden, walk toward the wide windows and peek in at the swimming pool. No one is there. No Huldra 8 with tubes, no TR 1040 amplifier with its warm tone, no jig. A downpour breaks the summer silence and settles on rooftops and leaves. From the other side of the windowpane we hear someone whisper: "Hush, now hush, and the loveliest sound will arise."

BEFORE JAPAN TOOK OVER

You must get past four guards before you can get in. At your left on the stairwell, Xenakis' one eye stares vaguely at you. Krzysztof Penderecki towers behind dark sunglasses when you come up to the second storey, and Finn Mortensen peers out through a window acting as though he does not notice you. On the way up to the third floor you run into the fatherly gaze of John Cage. The door to your goal now lays directly before you, though an ominous Olle Bærtling sculpture – or perhaps it's a geometrically shaped booby trap – is lurking just beside it.

I am in an industrial area near the centre of Oslo which houses the acoustic chamber of art collector and entrepreneur Erling Neby. Seen from above, from a Google satellite perspective, the functionalist building looks like a human ear, which means that I now must be standing in the middle of the ear canal. After ascending the stairs, past Tom Sandberg's monumental photographs, I arrive at a room 200 square meters in dimension. A room filled with one of Europe's largest collections of English and American tube amplifiers and loudspeakers from 1960 up until – as the head person himself says: "Japan took over the whole shebang."

Erling Neby began as an apprentice at the Tandberg Radio Factory in 1966. Three years later, he started up his own import business operating out of his flat in Lambertseter in Oslo. His 45 years of selling hi-fi products from Marantz, McIntosh, James B. Lansing Sound, INC., Nagra, Harmon Kardon, Tivoli and Geneva, have financed the accumulation of an internationally respected collection of concrete and geometrical art. In parallel, but much less well known and recognized, is Neby's other collection which he gleaned from following announcements in hi-fi magazines and sales lists sent via telefax and fax from foreign second hand merchants.

For a person who is more than slightly obsessed with music, modern art and industrial design, this place is put together so that *you* in particular will fall victim to Stendhals syndrome, a condition that causes individuals to keel over when they come into contact with particularly gorgeous art. For the first half an hour I walk around the room with a strained bladder, I refuse to waste valuable time on such basic needs. The right wall is covered with glass shelves upon which 120 tube amplifiers have been placed, while the left side comprises a nearly complete selection of high-end JBL loudspeakers. Three smaller alcoves house a vinyl collection, and extraordinary turntables that seem to resemble either walruses, canons or *paleolithic* insects. The industrial products also have a personal history: Here are two McIntosh MC3500 amplifiers which formed a part of the Wall of Sound formation for the band Grateful Dead and a Radford amplifier from Olympic Studios in England. Arne Nordheim's Torrentz TD 124-record player and JBL 1212 loudspeakers snooze in the corner. An EMT record player, developed for radio stations to be able to play 18" vinyl records, seems somewhat hapless standing in the middle of the room. The crown jewel of the collection, is the Steinway grand piano from Arne Bendiksen Studios, upon which the classic solo albums by Chick Corea, Keith Jarrett and Paul Bley were recorded. Because the stairway was too narrow, the piano had to be hoisted in with a crane after Neby had portions of the wall cut away.

Among this hi-fi landscape, other objects that stand out are a Aase Texmon Rygh, some Pipistrello lamps and scattered sculptures by Bård Breivik. A Jan Groth tapestry and Paul Osipow paintings function as symbolic sound mufflers. Even if Neby says that nothing sensible can be said about the relationship between the two collections, there are in fact several commonalities. Whether by an artistic hand or from the assembly line, good craftsmanship runs throughout each, be it a Korsmo or a Quad. Both collections have a functional and geometric design – anyone claiming to see the difference between Arnold Wolf's Paragon loudspeakers and a modern sculpture by Isamu Noguchi is lying. The tactile nature of Guzman's sculptures or Cruz-Diez's paintings are comparable to the physical sound produced by a McIntosh amplifier.

When I entered, the room seemed brutal. The absence of sound, or to be more precise, the presence of suppressed sound, reminds me of a natural history museum, in which creatures bob about in jars of formaldehyde. But I put on a record. With the help of two Project Everest DD66000 loudspeakers hooked up to a McIntosh MC 1,2 KW-amplifier, the room stirs to life. It becomes a geometrical symphony of teak, glass, metal, textiles and polished steel.

BOLLYWOOD ROCK

January 2011 was the coldest month that Delhi had experienced in 30 years. As the thermometer creeps down toward four degrees Celsius and the Himalayan winds rush freely along Edwin Lutyen's parade streets, India's capital city shuts down. Schools and official offices are closed, and on street corners people light up bonfires from rubbish and rubber tires to keep warm. All of which creates a thick blanket of smog above the city through which the sun cannot penetrate – in this way winter maintains its firm hold on Delhi. And in what might resemble a fictional scene from a Mad Max vs. The Road Bollywood film, the record stores stay wide open. Among the bazaars in the old city, one discovers record shops existing in a time vacuum; they forgot to switch to cassette tapes and CDs and still sell nothing but vinyl. In Meena Bazaar, shop no. 256, directly between the market's used car and sewing machine vendors, is Shah Music Centre, in business since 1928. A mere rickshaw ride away, you can find the Shah family's storage building with over 120 000 vinyl albums. This is where you drink darjeeling and listen to the world's largest collection of Hindu music, with your own private record clerk and duster. Only a short walk away, in the main street of Chandni Chowk that leads up to the Red Fort, there is another mainstay, Guru Kirpa Enterprises. This is where the eighty-year-old sikh, Blwant Singh has sold records for 52 years.

In Singh's 200-rupee stacks, you are able to find a ghazal LP of Ustad Amir Khan or the rare record by Bhimsen Joshi for which your Indian great uncle has long been searching. Western crate-diggers travel here, but also music dwellers from all of India. Littering the 300-rupee piles are all of the classic Bollywood soundtracks. From R.D. Burman's *The Burning Train* and *Shalimar* to Kalyanji Anandji's *Don* and *Commander*. Among the 400-rupee albums are those by Bappi Lahiri, India's disco and electro godfather, who is in demand for his Bollywood-izing of western artists such as Michael Jackson and The Buggles – long before global copyright laws were around. No one other than this master thief Lahiri would think to steel Herbie Hancock's *Rock It* and Tyrone Brunson's *The Smurf* in one and the same tune. At the very back of Singh's black storage unit, in the 500-rupee box, you discover the productions of Ananda Shankar.

The original raga-rocker, Ananda Shankar (1942—1999) was the nephew of the better well known Pandit Ravi Shankar. Rather than coasting along on his uncle's coattails, his wish, according to the debut album's liner notes, was to "...combine western and Indian music into a new form, music with no particular name, but which is without melody and captivating, one that combines the most modern electronic tricks with the old traditional instrument, the sitar." Ananda wanted to create the sound of 1960s modern India. He wasn't the first to foster such thoughts. In the mid-1960s, western rock bands such as The Kinks, Yardbirds and The Beatles incorporated imported tablas and sitars in their soundscapes and formed the basis for raga-rock. This trend spread to jazz within the more refined indo jazz genre that John Mayer, Alice Coltrane and Mahavishnu Orchestra operated within. Ananda Shankar was immediately hailed as the wunderkind of Asian rock when he visited Los Angeles in 1970. He shared the stage in LA with Jimi Hendrix, and with Reprise Records, he released his debut album, which contained covers of *Jumpin' Jack Flash* and *Light My Fire.* Shankar rode out his success for as long as he was able, and toured throughout the USA and Europe giving a stage show that offered traditional Indian dance combined with psychedelic light effects. It's thus not very surprising that his more conservative uncle became this nephew's toughest critic, maintaining that the crossover-technique watered down the traditional Indian culture. Ravi should probably have considered this before he invited George Harrison over for tea in 1966.

It wasn't until Ananda Shankar moved back home in 1975 and was signed at EMI India that he would create his major work, *Ananda Shankar and His Music*. While the USA debut sounded polished and well suited for Haight-Ashbery market studies, Shankar's homeland received the more intense Bollywood sound overridden with moogs, a string orchestra from Calcutta thrown in and infernally unbalanced drums – all of which was recorded with a single suspended microphone hanging from the roof in the studio. As the magical song *Streets of Calcutta* kicks off, it sounds like Klaus Schulze,

Led Zeppelin and an Indian sitarist caught together aboard a ghost ship sailing the seventh sea, and on which they are required to cook up the ultimate rock song in order to land in port.

THE RUBÁIYÁT OF DOROTHY ASHBY

Dorothy Ashby (1932—1986) is forever doomed to stand in the shadow of history's other great jazz harpist, Alice Coltrane. Even though Ashby currently appears as a mere footnote among an obscure footnote genre, jazz harp, most people have nonetheless heard her glissandos. Ashby was a studio musician on Stevie Wonder's *Songs in the Key of Life* and in the last decade her sounds have been revived by hip-hop producers such as Madlib and DJ Premier. Just as Joanna Newsom renewed the folk genre with her harp and voice in the early 2000s, Ashby employed the same weapon to create her highly personal folk interpretation of jazz in the 1960s.

When Dorothy Ashby debuted with Regent Records in 1957, she was met with strong resistance among jazz circles. The harp at that time was still a symbol of classical music, and its tone too esoteric to fit into the prevailing hard-bop of the day. But the record company gave Ashby the opportunity, with the hope to market her as the exotic jazz harpist and thereby be able to swallow up entire portions of the muzak market. And thus the jazz harp genre was born, the three-headed troll of chamber music, bop and exotica, and Ashby's early albums were given the most titillating titles like *The Jazz Harpist, Hip*

Harp, and *The Fantastic Jazz Harp*. Across the cover of the albums were photos of harps, harps, and more harps.

Ashby's escape from the yoke of jazz harp came when she signed on with the Chicago-based Cadet Records. The company's house producers, Richard Evans and Charles Stepney, had been shaping signature sounds for artists like Terry Callier, Rotary Connection, and Marlena Shaw since the mid 1960s, sounds at the intersection of symphonic soul and rock. Latching onto soul's grand string arrangements and backbeat drums, the duo combined the sound with a myriad of jazz musicians on vibraphones, guitar, flute and sax. By using a few overhead microphones in the Ter-Mar studio, the producers were able to create a sound hallmarked by extreme dynamism and subdued pathos, reminiscent of Jean-Claude Vannier, Jack Nitzsche and Willie Mitchell's orchestral arrangements for Hi Records. It is big, but sounds as if it's been recorded in a warm basement room in Chicago on a Sunday morning. When the Cadet's response to The Funk Brother's, the studio band The Soulful Strings, released the Christmas album *The Magic of Christmas* in 1968, Evans and Stepney showed that the Cadet sound could be adapted to any kind of material. Songs like *Jingle Bells* and *Santa Claus is Coming to Town* sound like they were originally written by Stepney and Evans for an unknown chubby white bearded soul artist from the north pole.

The first two albums that Dorothy Ashby released with Cadet were *Afro Harping* in 1968 and *Dorothy's Harp* in 1969. Richard Evans pulled Ashby more and more toward the direction of soul, and she had her first hit with the forceful psychedelic instrumental *Soul Vibrations*. When Ashby showed up one day at the Ter-Mar studio with two newly written songs based on poems by the Persian poet Omar Khayyám (1048–1131), Evan's first reaction was that she had to develop this into a full-scale conceptual album. This led Ashby to a deeper study of Edward FitzGerald's classical translation *The Rubáiyát of Omar Khayyám* from 1859, and she wrote ten compositions inspired by his epigrams. In order to fit the material, Ashby exchanged her harp for the Japanese stringed instrument, koto, and for the African thumb piano kalimba. She also chose to debut as a vocalist in her older age, and interpreted Khayyám's poetry both in the form of songs of praise and as meditative recitation. Richard Evans taking Ashby's cue, delivered some of his most astonishing arrangements for string tuned to an eastern scale, and made complete with sprawling, untamed percussion.

The album, *The Rubáiyát of Dorothy Ashby* from 1970, reflects Alice Coltrane's spiritual inversion from the albums *Huntingham Ashram Monestary* and *Journey in Satchidananda*, but also has leanings toward the reckless psychedelics of Andalou Pop by Turkish artists such as Ersen and Selda Bagcan. The resulting *Rubáiyát* exists today as a murky musical witch's brew, compared to which Morticia Addams' culinary skills seem like raw food. If you're ever to be told on the street that jazz harp is dead, you should turn around and reply: "Dear sirs, that genre is alive and well, as much as French horn house or accordion disco. Open your ears, you numbskull!"

ODE TO THE LIGHT

One Norwegian property agent said to the other: “Oslo is the new New York!” The other replied: “Drammen is Dubai!” The third one yelled: “Tønsberg, after they build the new pier, is the new Miami!” The art historian, who also wishes to beat on relativism’s bass drum today, said: “Storedal Cultural Centre in the town of Skjeberg, is the new Acropolis!”

Sitting in a broad, open valley, encircled by eastern Norway’s towering spruce forests, is Storedal Cultural Centre for the visually impaired. The centre, which opened in 1970, was initiated and financed by the musician, human rights activist and philanthropist Erling Stordahl (1923—1994). He himself became blind as a thirteen-year-old, and dedicated large portions of his adult life to proving that this disability was not a hindrance, but rather an opportunity for self-expression. After reaching the top of the Norwegian accordion championships at the age of 15, he formed a duo with the visually impaired singer, Gunnar Engedahl. Together they churned out classics like *Måkenes Vals* (The Waltz Of The Seagulls) and *Minnenes Melodi* (Memory’s Melody) over which many a grandmother has sighed into her Huldra radio device. All royalties from their albums and concert honoraria were paid directly to Norway’s Association for the Blind.

In the 1960s, Stordahl became engaged in the integration of the visually impaired within sports. He arranged ski trips and mountain treks for the blind, in order to show that a person could develop other senses and methods for observing nature. His work was crowned by the opening of *Ridderrennet* in 1962 (the world's largest annual winter sports tournament for the visually and motion impaired) and by the creation of the Beitostølen Health Sport Centre in 1970. When Stordahl overtook his family farm outside of Skjeberg near Sarpsborg, he wanted to build an experiential centre for the visually impaired dedicated to King Magnus the Blind. According to Snorri Sturluson's sagas, the somewhat peripheral prince Magnus was born in Storedal in 1117. From his earliest childhood days, he suffered from severe mental illness that threatened to lead him toward an inescapable doom. At the age of 20, he was thrown from his throne and handed over to Harald Gilles' men, who blinded and gelded him. Magnus converted and entered the monastery. Unlike historians, Erling Stordahl did not interpret the Magnus myth as a sad tragedy, but as an individual with a serious disability who overcame his difficulties in adversity. For it was only when he sat alone and blind that Magnus began to see the people around him and to understand his place in the world. Through the darkness, he discovered the path to light, and this has become the centre's motto.

Erling Stordahl commandeered several professors, scientists and artists to create the space. It would include a sense garden, a petroglyph park and an amphitheatre integrated into the landscape. But Stordahl was clear about one thing: the dominating impression should be a monumental work by the Norwegian modernist sculptor Arnold Haukeland of a magnificent replica of King Magnus' blind fate. Haukeland came up with a construction formed from two long, black, symmetrical rods that appear like a pair of confused arms outstretched toward heaven. Shooting out from between these black arms is a silver spear, a light reaching upward, overcoming powerlessness. Stordahl liked Haukeland's idea, and the work began. In the phase that followed, the composer Geir Tveitt was hired to set the tone of the park and sculpture, but the two artists soon began to collide on their ideas of the sculpture's abstract impression. Tveitt demanded that Haukeland carve some figurative reliefs at the base of the sculpture so that visitors could understand the Magnus-myth. When Haukeland deliberately broke every deadline, Tveitt pulled out of the project and wrote, enraged: "If the starting point is to be unclear and abstract, I have no faith in the viability of the artwork. The abstract artists may say what they like and overestimate their fantasy until they turn blue in the face." But the work continued, and in 1965, the avant garde composer Arne Nordheim entered the project as a replacement for Tveitt. Haukeland and Nordheim soon found a common tone and began to imagine sound as an integrated part of the sculpture. The vision was that variations of light and weather patterns at Storedal should influence the distribution of Nordheim's sound out through the sculpture's 26-metre-high loud speakers. In addition, Nordheim's tones should reflect the materials that Haukeland had used; iron and stainless steel. Haukeland and Nordheim claimed that the visually impaired would thus be offered a full artistic experience in meeting the sculpture. The blind would see.

During the period from 1965—1968, Arne Nordheim worked together with engineers from the Acoustic Laboratory at NTH in Trondheim in order to realise the technical aspects of the work. In a letter to Stordahl's secretary and friend, Otto Johansen, Nordheim wrote quite poetically about the ongoing work: "We are the ones who will decide how the machine should work. That is also art." The solution was to equip the surface of the sculpture with a number of photoelectric cells that registered light in the landscape. Depending on the varying seasons and time of day, the cells would always convey new impulses that would influence the electronic music playing from two tapes. Another breakthrough was when Haukeland developed a large, floating ring made of stainless steel around the middle of the sculpture. This was where Nordheim would mount the majority of the 26 loud speakers, thereby spreading the sound into the landscape, enabling visually impaired visitors to follow the forms, distances and directions in the sculpture. The result was that Nordheim's electronic tones mingled with the sounds of nature and thundered out across the landscape. The farmers in Skjeberg thought a cosmonaut had made an emergency landing in their fields. On his debut album, Nordheim rightfully wrote: "This Record should be played loud." And quite rightly, after a few months, Stordahl was forced to dampen the volume when local authorities claimed that it frightened birds and wildlife in the area. Today, *Ode To The Light* is a hidden pearl in Norwegian art history; a meeting between two giants of Norwegian modernism and one of the first close collaborative projects between artists and engineers. Storedal Cultural Centre is opened seasonally in July and August each year, so plan your family trip this summer and get sound art and ice cream in one scoop!

P.S.! It may not be the best idea to bring along your visually impaired friend. In a newly rediscovered documentary, *The Sound Sculpture* (1970) from the NRK archives, one can watch several interviews with visually impaired people about their experiences with *Ode to The Light*. In complete contrast to the artists' ambitions, most of them shake their heads in exasperation, and say that the sculpture is incomprehensible – as though a German vehicle of war has settled down in a field in Skjeberg.

RAGE IN BUENOS AIRES

Over the past decade, forgotten oddities have been excavated by music archaeologists throughout the world. In the same way that the Smithsonian, Nonsuch, Bärenreiter and WERGO record companies commendably documented ethnological music in the 1960s, small indie labels such as Buda Music, Honest Jons, Art Yard and Finders Keepers have continued this work by unearthing everything from iron curtain jazz to *compas* from Haiti. It's no coincidence that the history of music is written from a western viewpoint. Just as our forefathers smuggled out an obelisk or two in their suitcases home from Luxor, a hand full of Englishmen and Japanese in the early 1980s sucked up record labels and overstocked music all over the world, sending home containers bursting with cheap LPs. Posted for awhile on a record forum for nerds, www.soulstrut.com, was a fairly enjoyable map. This portrayed, following the same principles that the colonial lords used to divide up Africa with a ruler during the Berlin conference in 1884, how western record collectors and DJs have laid claim to the music history of various countries. I suspect that if the London-based record company Whatmusic.com had partaken in the fictitious conference, they would have drawn a large red circle around Argentina.

Argentina's proud European traditions and strong Latin American roots have led to a rich musical inheritance that reaches out beyond Carlos Gardel's *Volver* and Astor Piazzolla's *nuevo tango.* In addition to international names such as Lalo Schiffrin, Dino Saluzzi and Gato Barbieri, Argentina has also hosted an exquisite local jazz scene. The record company Whatmusic.com has reissued Argentinian nuggets like the tenor saxophone Haracio "Chivo" Borraro's modal jazz classic *El Nuevo Sonido Del Chivo Borraro* (1966) and Alberto Favero's *Suite Trane* (1968), a requiem dedicated to John Coltrane. In 2004, they released the crown jewel of the Argentinian catalogue, Jorge López Ruiz's masterpiece *Bronca Buenos Aires* (Rage In Buenos Aires), which had originally been released by Trova Records in 1971.

Although Buenos Aires, with its world record density of psychoanalysts, might bring to mind a southern European metropolis from the 1960s, time does not pause here either. In 1966, the political climate between right and left in Argentina had become so acidic that assassinations, kidnappings and bomb explosions almost happened on a daily basis. The country's innocence vanished with its dirty war, and Argentina's music shifted. This made an especially strong impression on the young composer and bassist, Jorge López Ruiz (1935-), who had defined a new generation on the Argentinian jazz scene with his album *B.A. Jazz* from 1961. Affected by the era's gravitas, he recorded his first political album, *El Grito* (The Scream) in 1966, a work directly inspired by the military coup and deposition of the legally elected president Arturo Umberto Illia in that year. His political engagement increased, and in 1971, López Ruiz entered the well known ION studio in Buenos Aires to record the follow up album, *Bronca Buenos Aires*. The album was based on the civil uprising against the military in the city of Córdoba in May 1969, later referred to colloquially as *El Cordobazo,* and López Ruiz later wrote that the album quietly reflected "a society that has lost its freedom, and what's worse, the dignity of its own life and work."

In the four-piece jazz suite, with the subtitles *The Empty City, Tales, Love Buenos Aires* and *Rage Buenos Aires*, López Ruiz joined forces with the young Argentinian poet José Tcherkaski who recites his own politically laden and vibrant poetry. Even though I don't understand the words, his voice is so calm, safe and insistent that you are certain they will win their case. Together with heavyweights like Chivo Borraro, Fernando Gelbard and Carlos "Pocho" Lapouble, as well as a 19-man band and choir, López Ruiz presented monumental big band jazzrock hinting at both Gary McFarland's *America the Beautiful* and Gil Evan's *Svengali*. With its flame-red cover depicting a stone-throwing student, *Bronca Buenos Aires* stands alongside Charlie Haden's *Liberation Music Orchestra* and Public Enemy's *Fear of a Black Planet* as a symbol of how music can break free of the abstract tonal world and have an impact on the tax and blood pressures of a society's citizens. The album provides glimpses of courage and hope, but is laden with depression. It is like a political ballad sung with too much immersion, which you will never quite be able to get out of your head.

MULTIMAL – JAZZ & POETRY IN NORWAY 1960—1980

The Jazz and Poetry genre was born in the USA at the end of the 1950s. Bebop and beat poetry had provided the key to a popular modernism that was able to overthrow desk poets and release the post war generation's howl. The J&P genre as we know it began with Kenneth Rexroth and Lawrence Ferlinghetti's readings at the San Francisco club *The Cellar* in the spring of 1957. Most likely the first J&P meeting took place long before this; in a nightclub where an unknown poet happened to read a poem above the tones of a just-as-obscure jazz musician, without those in attendance feeling as though they had just witnessed the birth of a new genre. Words and music have always had a symbiotic relationship, from Greek odes and West African griot traditions to Iceberg Slim's spoken word and Biz Markie's rap. But at *The Cellar*, bebop-jazz and beat poetry were presented together for the first time, an artistic genre found its character and expression in the interaction between jazz musicians and poets, music and text, improvisation and recitation, artists and the public.[32] And when these individual elements were suddenly forged together, one witnessed the birth of a new genre. J&P contains the seeds for seeking out popular modernism. The jazz would save poetry from academia so that together they could realise political liberation.[33] The beat poets had finally located the secret weapon for achieving the goal in their fight against the analytical and modernistic Eliot/Pound tradition. As Rexroth wrote: "If we can get poetry out into the life of the country, it can be creative. Homer, or the guy who recited Beowulf, was show business. We simply want to make poetry part of 'show business.'"[34]

During the 1950s, the spread of the jazz bug in the USA began to reach its peak, the same bug that would reach Norway a few years later in mutated form. Each week, a new jazz hit was broadcast on the radio, in most cities it was possible to go see jazz opera or jazz ballet on Saturday nights, or why not buy a jazz book written by a jazz poet deeply inspired by the blue, blue, blue jazz? Young people weren't flocking to American Apparel to find a new uniform but rather dug their grandfathers' old tweed suits out of mothballs. You didn't post your twerk dance on YouTube, but instead frequented a dance party to showcase your new jazz moves. And one and two, and one, two, three, four.

With the entry of bebop into jazz, the music's harmonies and structures became too complicated to pair with "normal" lyrics. Attempts were made to salvage the vocals with scatting or vocalese, but bebop remained an instrumental genre. However, the beat poets discovered that the poetry which they wished to write, filled with what would later become the archetypal modern tools and ideas of post war lyrics, combined superbly with bebop's rhythms, improvisation and tone. Back to the street level: *The Cellar* in San Francisco was packed night after night by people hoping to check out the new phenomenon. J&P readings spread across the entire USA, particularly on the west coast and in New York. Record companies were eager to follow up with several LP releases in 1957 and 1958 with Lonnie Elder/Charlie Mingus[35], Jack Kerouac/Steve Allen[36], Langston Hughes/Red Allen and Charles Mingus[37], and Leonard Feather. The evenings at *The Cellar* were compiled on the cult record *Poetry Readings in the Cellar*[38], released on the San Francisco label, Fantasy Records.

The link between the beat and bebop culture and the simple *do-it-yourself* attitude – find a bassist and read a poem! – helped the genre to spread wildly throughout student and jazz communities. But there was one disadvantage: the idea was much better than its execution. A lack of self-critique among those who practiced the style in fact hindered the development of the genre and muddied the artistic goals, and after its novelty wore off in a few years, the phenomenon vanished from the USA. But J&P had already spread to other countries. In Scandinavia, the young poet Matts Rying read at the Moderna Museet in Stockholm with Hacke Björksten's orchestra, and at the Fiolteateret in Copenhagen, the soon to become film director Jørgen Leth recited the poem *Warszawa* together with vibraphonist Louis Hjulmand.

'THIS IS MEANINGFUL! THIS IS CONNECTION!'

On the evening of February 22, 1960, J&P came to Norway. The student society at the National Academy of Craft and Art Industry in Oslo presented Norway's first J&P evening during which the students Arne Sundland and Per Fosser had requested permission from the poets Erling Christie, Harald Sverdrup and Paal Brekke to recite their works. The musicians, Arild Wikstrøm, Finn Eriksen, Bjørn Johansen, Knut Høiland, Bjørn Mortensen and Ole Jacob Hansen accompanied. The locale was packed when Sundland began with a version of Christie's poem, *Jailhouse Rock* and Wikstrøm played a monotonous blues with elements of boogie-woogie. The audience held their breath until the last sounds – and words – faded out. The arrangement was declared a success in *Dagbladet* the next morning, and the young journalist Jan Erik Vold claimed that it left one with a taste for more: "Not everything was equally successful, it's true, but a few of the numbers showed the kinds of possibilities for such collaboration between poetry and jazz."[39]

The spring of 1962 saw the first regular J&P readings in Oslo at the Studenterkroa (Student Pub) in Storgata, held as part of The Norwegian Student's Association *Unpopular Evening* series. For two years, the evenings were arranged in various locales throughout Oslo. The initiators were a gang centred around the Student Theatre who viewed themselves in opposition to a Norway that was characterized by Håkon Lie, the cultivation of housewives, and the fact that one could count the capital city's total number of night clubs on one hand with two fingers cut off. The movement unpacked its identity by the simultaneous cultivation of poetry and jazz, and in the somewhat odd assortment of people one could find characters like Kate

Næss, Stein Mehren, Noel Cobb, Karin Krog, Ellen Refsdal, Ulrikke Greve, Attila Horvath, Janken Varden and Dag Åkeson Moe, with the jazz and blues pianist Arild Wikstrøm as the fixed conductor.[40] A handwritten memo penned by Noel Cobb lists the programme for one *Unpopular Evening* in the spring of 1963. Over the course of one night, Ellen Refsdal recites the poem *The Moon* by Federico García Lorca and *Rue de Seine* by Jacques Prévert. Karin Krog takes on *Please* and *Oh No* by the American poet Robert Creeley, while Ulrikke Greve reads *When You Are Gone* (*Når du er borte*) and *To Unnamed* (*Til ein namnlaus*) by Tor Jonsson. Stein Mehren recites his own poems *Landscape with Snow (Landskap med sne)*, *Metropol* and *Of Consequences (Av konsekvenser)* and Noel Cobb concludes by reading *My Narrow Bed*.

Compared to the segregated mothership, the USA, Norway was a place where it was difficult to find meaning and opposition. One evening, some of the musicians went up to Sentrum Scene to buy hash, they hang around at Studentkroa and fire up in the middle of the bar. But no one in the place even noticed, because no one in Oslo knew what hash was; they simple thought it smelled like rotten tobacco. For those involved, however, their actions were just as symbolic as cigarettes in the 1800s. Before inhaling, they say together: "This is meaningful. This is connection!"[41]

Throughout the 1960s, a series of J&P recordings and arrangements illustrate the spread of the genre. In November 1963, the TV programme *Vi unge* (We Youthful) was shown in which six poems by Jan Erik Vold are recited by actress Tone

Schwarzott above the sound of abstract tones and jazz music for a trio, composed by Svein Erik Børja. In the spring of 1964, film director Arild Kristo arranged a *photo-poetry-jazz-evening* in the University Concert Hall with Arild Wikstrøm's orchestra. In January 1966, the guitarist Robert Normann played on NRK as the actors Sverre Wilberg and Kari Simonsen recited six poems by Magli Elster, Herman Wildenvey, Hans Børli, Erling Christie, Ernst Orvil and Louis Kvalstad. In June of the same year, a programme called *Ord og Rytme* (Word and Rhythm) was broadcast, in which the musicians Earl Wilson, Arild Wikstrøm, Jostein Hetland, Helge Vetå and Ole J. Johansen play as poet Tone Ringen and author Sigmund Jakobsen read aloud. In March 1967, Robert Normann returned to the airwaves, this time with Karin Krog who interprets the poem *Selvbiografi* (Autobiography) by Swedish poet Sonja Åkesson.[42] One highlight of this period is a tour by the Riksteatret in 1969, with a constellation that called itself *Jazzhouse*. Poets Harald Sverdrup, Halldis Moren Vesaas, and Gunnar Bull Gundersen joined forces with jazz musicians Espen Rud, Calle Neumann, Ivar Antonsen, Bjørn Alterhaug, Ditlef Eckhoff and Laila Dalseth. There is no sound or photo documentation of this collaboration, apart from the vague memories about the enormous contrast between Sverdrup and Gundersen's brutal and striking readings and Vesaas' meditative, quiet recitation above Neumann's saxophone solo. With so many strong personalities on the same tour bus, it wasn't long before there were fireworks, something which led to Guri Vesaas replacing her mother until the group disbanded in 1971.

FROM WHITE TO WHITE – JAN ERIK VOLD AND JAN GARBAREK THROUGH THE DECADE

In 1959, a twenty-year-old aspiring author and journalist by the name of Jan Erik Vold is walking around Fagerborg dreaming of writing novels like Johan Borgen. He digs jazz, is a sworn Lester Young fan and has recently begun writing freelance for *Dagbladet*. He later claimed that he was always more comfortable with musicians than with authors. "Do you know why? Because musicians can't win the Nobel Prize."[43] Vold became the first promoter of J&P in Norway through several of his articles published in *Dagbladet* from 1959 to 1964 with their somewhat unwieldy titles: "Poetry and jazz fuse together – Young artists in the USA recite lyrics accompanied by jazz music"[44] "Can jazz boost authors' literary accomplishments?"[45]; "Poetry and jazz – an exciting meeting between two art forms,"[46]; and let's not forget, "Can jazz and poetry meet?"[47] The articles provide a firsthand impression of the history of the fledgling genre and its difficult birth in the USA and Norway. Vold addresses basic challenges, such as the lack of synchronicity in poetry and jazz, the imbalance in the fact that the poets most often depend on support from the jazz musicians, and not the other way around. He also asks whether modern poetry is merely drowning in its meeting with the music. At the same time, Vold emphasizes that in its good moments, J&P can supplement both jazz and poetry with a new dimension that becomes an entity in and of itself. His debut as a J&P reader occurs one evening in 1966 after he and the Finnish poet and jazz pianist Claes Andersson decide to throw a spontaneous concert at the

Studentkroa pub in Oslo, at which Vold recites Andersson's poems, whilst the latter plays the piano.

So it's no mere coincidence when, on Tuesday, July 30, 1969, producer Svein Eirk Børja runs to Mikkel Aas, a representative for the record label Philips, with the poetry collection *Mor Godhjertas glade versjon. Ja* tucked under an arm, after having seen Jan Erik Vold reading at the Molde cinema during the annual jazz festival. He proposes producing a J&P recording with Vold and Jan Garbarek as quickly as humanly possible. Børja is familiar with the poet's relationship with the genre and jazz music in general, and knows that Vold is in vogue after the release of *Mor Godhjerta*. Across the country, people have begun to notice the characteristic voice that reads the "hit" poems "Funny" and "Tale for Loffen" (Speech for The White Bread). Jan Garbarek is starting to become well known internationally and has worked closely with jazz singer Karin Krog. There have been rumours that his new quartet has been signed on with the German record company Edition of Contemporary Music (ECM). Mikkel Aas likes the idea – at last, the momentum and opportunities have arisen to promote a J&P record in Norway.

On a day in autumn in 1969, Jan Erik Vold makes his way toward Gamlebyen where Garbarek lives, unknown territory for a boy from Fagerborg. They sit together all evening long exchanging ideas about the music that should be recorded on the album and go through *Mor Godhjerta* to choose poems. On October 16, Vold and Garbarek meet in the studio, where the quartet from Molde (with Terje Rypdal, Jon Christensen and Arild Andersen), together with producer Svein Erik Børja are ready and waiting. But Vold and the musicians do not enter the studio together, he is not quite comfortable reading synchronistically with the musicians, and Børja has the idea that Vold should record the readings alone in the studio room while the quartet sits outside at the mixing table. Afterwards, Børja rigs up four sets of headphones for the musicians, and with Vold in their ears, they play as Børja controls Vold's voice from the tape player. The resulting LP is *Briskeby Blues*, which was released in November 1969, Norway's first J&P recording. The A-side of the LP features Vold reciting the long poem *Bo på Briskeby Blues* (Living at Briskeby Blues) without music, while the B-side holds thirteen of Vold's poems over Garbarek's own compositions – the first grooves that ever show the particular Vold/Garbarek style. Garbarek has strayed away from John Coltrane, but at the same time buys into half of the Impulse! and Flying Dutchman catalogues with Pharoah Sanders and Gato Barbieri. The music is interspersed with Vold's warm, original voice that is reminiscent of cool jazz. Both the music and the listening experience are of the highest quality and succeed in being elevated to a higher realm. For example, in the song *Tang* (Seaweed), in which Arild Andersen's thick, hypnotic bass line calls to mind kelp and seaweed that is bashed against the reef in the Oslo fjord, and Garbarek's tone feels like the sun light warming the entire shoreline so that one can smell the tangy seaweed. The LP receives much attention in the news, with remarks varying from raging blind tributes to commentaries calling the collaboration "bearded high culture!"[48] On January 7,

1970, the LP reaches spot number 19 on the VG music chart. Two weeks later, it's climbed to number 13, and the week thereafter, the LP reaches its zenith in tenth place.

Mikkel Aas and Philips strike while the iron is hot and decide to follow up the LP as quickly as possible. In September 1970, the Garbarek quartet is in Arne Bendiksen's studio with Manfred Eicher recording the classic album *Afric Pepperbird*. The next week, the quartet meets up again in the same studio dragging along Swedish pianist Bobo Stenson, Jan Erik Vold and Svein Erik Børja to record the follow up to *Briskeby Blues*: the LP album *HAV* (SEA). Producer Børja pronounces that they are not going to copy the spontaneous success of *Briskeby Blues*, but promises that they should attempt to "arrive at a full integration of the elements of word-music and thereby create a new audio style".[49] Once again, Vold goes in first and records his vocals. The musicians enter directly afterwards, this time equipped with headphones and stop watches in order to know the precise moment when Vold's vocals start. The soundscape is updated to create a thicker tapestry, woven by Stenson's electric piano and Rypdal's fuzz guitar. Christensen is an inconstant metronome that fits perfectly with the music's inner beats. After the recording, Børja remains in the studio to mix the album. He wants to strike the perfect balance between voice and music. After several costly days, he is finally satisfied, but this time even the album cover should be perfect as part of a larger whole. Vold argues with the record company, insisting that the cover should portray Odd Geir Sæther's large green coloured photos of the sea and rocks. *HAV* is released in January of 1971, and is in many ways a more unified album than *Briskeby Blues*. Vold's poetry seems to be made to fit the music this time. The musicians and the poet are no longer struggling against each other but playing toward one another. This is best exemplified in the 21-minute-long track *Dikt* (Poem), in which the band plays for 17 minutes and 34 seconds before Vold enters with four lines before vanishing once again. It is both subtle and powerful. *HAV* is received with even higher praise than its predecessor, resulting in extensive tours. In March 1972, Jan Erik Vold and the Jan Gabarek Trio tour 37 Oslo schools, presenting one hour of poetry and jazz. The NRK broadcasts the entire occasion and the J&P genre is spread throughout all of Norway's flickering wooden TV boxes.

In 1972, Vold publishes a translation of the American lyricist Robert Creely's poem *Everything is water/if you look long enough* in the Paxlyrikk series. When he discovers that Creeley is heading to Berlin in August of the same year, he arranges for the American poet to take a trip to Norway in September. Between lectures and readings in Oslo and Bergen, they make a radio recording where the poets alternately read original texts and translations. However, Vold's secret plan to record an album with pianist Egil Kapstad and Robert Creeley is never realized. Some months later, when the head of the radio theatre, Gerhard Knoop, calls Vold up to ask whether he and Garbarek could make a production, Vold decides to record a J&P broadcast of Creely's poem – perhaps this time it will result in an album?

But before going to NRK, Vold/Garbarek have a full schedule. In 1973, the *Tram Campaign* has started in Oslo, fighting against the city council's movement to shut down Oslo's four remaining tram lines. The rabble rouser Vold is replaced with community activist Vold, and he brings Garbarek into the studio to record an EP on Philip's called *Tramlines / Three small things.* In November of the same year, Vold and the new Garbarek/Stenson quartet set out on a new national concert circuit with 50 events. When one listens to these recordings, it is clear that Vold is starting to become freer and freer with the music. Before each concert, he arranges a large table on the stage on which he places books with his own poetry collections and his translations of William Carlos Williams, Peter Bichsel, Bob Dylan and Robert Creeley. During the concerts, he improvises with which poem he will read and selects the pieces at random from a book. Vold is drawing closer to the idea that the reader is also a musician. Directly after the conclusion of their tour, the Garbarek quartet goes into Arne Bendiksen's studio to record *Witchi-Tai-To* with Manfred Eicher. In February 1974, the quartet shows up at the NRK studios at Marienlyst together with Vold to record the radio broadcasts *Love, Rain* in which some of the melodies from the *Witchi-Tai-To* album are used to set the tone for Creeley's poem. The recording is aired on July 1 of the same year, and Jan Erik Vold writes in NRK's programme guide:

> Love, Rain. What does it mean? That it is raining on our love – or: if you don't have love, at least you have rain? (or at least rain exists). There are several open possibilities, the most important thing (we might say) is that there are possibilities here, there are

openings. And so it goes the way that it goes, in life, in love – that which is soft, and wet, and rainy: is important to bring along on the journey, Creeley insists, as do we five who have brought you this programme... Altogether: 24 poems, 6 grooves. (Turn on your ears!)[50]

Alas no LP album is made; the 35-minute long recording is committed to tape, buried in NRK's archives at Marienlyst.

After a brief hiatus of three years, the Vold / Garbarek collaboration enter their final phase during the years of 1977—79. In September 1977, the band records its last record, the double album *Ingentings Bjeller* with the Garbarek / Stenson quartet, released by Norsk PolyGram. On this album, Garbarek and Vold take their collaboration to its final form and elevate the J&P genre to an artistic height. For the first time, Vold reads together with the musicians in the studio and the band produces the album themselves. The poet designs the cover, and with the exception of *Svingdør,* all of the poems are also printed for the first time on the album cover fold; the LP emerges as both a poetry collection and an album in one. The release becomes the subject of heated debate. NRK's radio programme *Grammoforum* plays a clip of *Skillingsvise* in which Vold addresses the media's coverage of the murder case *Berit from Karihaugen*, which had become the media's favourite case over the last year. NRK's programme director, Halfdan Hegtun, is called to put out the fires and prints a large red mark next to the song on the back side of the cover – *Skillingsvise* shall no longer be played on NRK.

In 1978, Vold and Garbarek receive an inquiry from Henie Onstad Kunstsenter's director Ole Henrik Moe and Merete Bergersen, the leader of Norway's first free dance troupe, Høvik Ballet. Would the duo like to put poetry and music to the commissioned work *White on White*, a ballet that is going to be produced to mark the art centre's 10-year celebration? Garbarek puts Håkon Graff on synthesizer and Jon Christensen on drums, and Vold writes a series of new poems based on the topic: the seasons from winter to winter, from white to white. On March 1, 1978, the piece is performed in front of a packed audience at the art centre, and seven dancers move to Vold and Garbarek's J&P. The show is an artistic success, and is followed up with extensive touring through Oslo and Akershus. In October 1979, the group is invited to give a concert at the University in Moscow organized by the Friendship Society of Norway-Soviet Union and The Norwegian Book Club. Russian students fill the hall and listen to Jan Erik Vold intoning in Norwegian to the saxophonist's characteristic, Nordic harmonies. While walking around Moscow's white streets, Vold and Garbarek know that their paths will soon part. Garbarek has a burgeoning international career that requires all of his time, and Vold has moved to Sweden and started a family. On Sunday, December 2, 1979, a notice printed in *Dagbladet* announces that Vold/Garbarek are to play between 6:45 and 7:00 pm. at the National Theatre, organized by the Norwegian Author Centre. This is to be their last known appearance together.

MULTIMAL – TROND BOTNEN AND THE SVEIN FINNERUD TRIO

In the spring of 1970, the visual artist Trond Botnen is putting the finishing touches on the last works that will be included in a new exhibition at Galleri Haaken. Gyldendal Publisher's editor in chief, Sigmund Hoftun, an old acquaintance of Botnen, is visiting to see his latest works, and he inquires in passing whether Botnen doesn't also write. Botnen admits that he has some old archived writing that are, from his perspective, purely hackwork, but hands over some pages that Hoftun takes with him. Later that same day, Hoftun calls to say that the so-called hackwork, which will later become the debut collection *Nattordbok* (Night Dictionary), has been accepted by Gyldendal. At the publisher's autumn book launch at the Continental in 1970, Trond Botnen sits deeply planted in a sofa drinking sherry after sherry and chatting with Gyldendal's director, Brikt Jensen. The publisher offhandedly sighs that he never has to print a second edition of a debut poetry collection. Botnen, pumped full of sherry by this point, wages a bet with the director. If *Nattordbok* sells so well that it warrants a second printing, the young poet will be allowed to paint a red cross on the ceiling of the director's office. Brikt Jensen accepts. The next morning, Botnen hatches a plan and calls up jazz pianist Svein Finnerud, an old mate from his etching course at the Art- and Crafts School in Oslo. He proposes collaborating on an artistic project, and an implied sales deal, which he dubs *Multimal*.

In 1970, Svein Finnerud was a well established graphic artist and jazz musician in the Norwegian art world. His trio, consisting of the bassist Bjørnar Andresen and drummer Espen Rud, was seen as one of the leading groups within Norwegian avant garde jazz. Through diverse collaborations with New Music composers Kåre Kolberg and Sigurd Berge, they had explored concrete music and graphic notation. With their musical theatre pieces *Revejakt i oppvaskkummen* (Fox Hunting in the Kitchen Sink) and *Poco. Coro. Corso.,* the trio had also become Norwegian exponents for happening- and performance art. The trio appeared on stage with grass clippers and exercise bikes, handed out percussion instruments to the audience, and raffled off cakes. The concerts weren't meant to be final products, but something procedural created through the interaction between the audience, the artists, and an array of coincidences. One such example of this way of thinking was the trio's participation in the happening *Kaleidoscope 67* in the Munch Museum, at which the university lecturer, Kjell Skyllstad's work *Abstraction 1* was performed. The title *gesamtkunstwerk* was nearly not expansive enough for all of the effects with which Skyllstad had armed the cannon. Live action painting? Check. Concrete music? Check. A reading of John Cage's *Lecture on Nothing*? Check. Ballet dancers? Check. Live video production? Check. Rotating psychedelic lights? Check. A specially designed canvas? Check. A mime theatre? Check. Improvisational jazz trio? Check there as well. The pathway to working with Trond Botnen and his *Multimal* project was not far away.

In the fall of 1970, Trond Botnen and Svein Finnerud travel together out to the Henie Onstad Kunstsenter and meet director Ole Henrik Moe.

They present *Multimal*, a multi-happening and attempt to solve a problem that is as old as various art forms – "to break down the barriers between them and form a fusion that seems natural and right."[51] Moe keeps his typical poker face, but at the end of the presentation, bursts out: "That's a brilliant idea!" For a director who had spent time earlier going out and actively seeking for cross-artistic collaborations, it was pure luck to have one drop right into his lap. He offers up both technical equipment and presentation space to be at their disposal.

There's not much that needs practicing; both Botnen and the trio possess a completely free-form mindset – everything will be improvised – whatever happens, happens. The only thing that must be clarified beforehand is the projection of the graphics. Another art school pal, the subsequently well known video artist Kjell Bjørgeengen, is given responsibility for projecting slides of various fragments of Finnerud's and Botnen's graphic works atop the band and readers. They decide that both of the artists' works should be projected on top of one another. On November 9, 1971, the studio hall is full as Botnen reads his bone dry, satirical poem to the trio's freebag-jazz, as Bjørgeengen works the projector. His unpretentious "hackwork" is perfectly suited to the trio's live performance. The slides that are presented are also completely new to the young people in the hall. Finnerud's trio has obviously been listening to Joe Zawinul's electronic arrangements for Miles Davis and Herbie Hancock's sextet. Svein Finnerud has swapped out the piano with a Rhodes, Andresen plays simple ostinato bass lines, and Espen Rud is channelling Tony Williams and Jack

DeJohnette. Above the soundscape, Botnens' nasal voice chants:

> When the gravity of hewn stone and bronze disappeared / it made problems for us all / across the entire city, the monuments took off / from their sockets and rose to the sky / SAS DC 9 Flight to London entered a meteorite shower of Norwegian bronze animals / such as hens; birds and small roe deer and plummeted weeping into the North Sea / the facade of the personal gallery was badly damaged by busts violently bursting their way to freedom / it was in many ways a catastrophic day / but it was a breathtaking sight to see Vigeland Sculpture Park vanish behind the horizon.

Inside the auditorium, a representative from the National Concert Organisation is liking what he is hearing. He books the project for a similar happening in the Munch Museum and on a subsequent tour through Norway. When the trio, Kjell Bjørgeengen and the poet Eivind Kahrs[52] arrive in Florø, they are informed that the arranged concert has been cancelled. The chairman Erik J. Evensen in Florø concert society explains the cancellation thus: "... We believe this is such a special gateway into modern music that we expect the public to react quite strongly. We would rather be condemned as reactionary than to be labelled as ones who accept everything." The trio starts up a spontaneous protest outside the hotel with posters and banners, and searches instead for a disco or gymnasium that can house the concert. On the following day, a crowded free concert is held at the local high school. All of the attention around *Multimal* and the extensive tours makes *Nattordbok* a commercial success, and a second edition must be printed. Wearing a barely-concealed grin across his face, Trond Botnen comes to Brikt Jensen's office at Gyldendal, and as the director holds the ladder, Botnen paints a large cross on the ceiling with red paint.

In 1971, Trond Botnen releases his second poetry collection *Gruver Toms hytte* (Miner Tom's Cabin), and in the same year, The Norwegian Book Club decides to release an LP with *Multimal*. Botnen, Finnerud and Andresen, together with drummer Svein Christiansen and saxophonist Carl Magnus Neumann, book themselves into Rosenborg studio at Fagerborg. Finnerud and Botnen have hand selected poems from Botnen's two collections, but no one has planned out what is going to happen musically. The only fixed point is that Andresen insists on using the bass line from Herbie Hancock's *Ostinato* in some place or other. This leads to an improvised recording, with Botnen jamming with and reading wherever it seems fitting, cracking up and reading on. They discover some old western pianos in the studio and order the sound technician to dig out any tapes with good sounds. "We want some seagull screams!" In the next minute, they are jamming over themes of *Silent Night* as the sound technician Leif Østby does his best to open the windows to let out the cloud of smoke. *Multimal* is released in the fall of 1971 on Polydor, and the first 1,500 copies are quickly sold out. When it's time for the album to be re-printed, the Book Club discovers that they've lost the master tapes, and *Multimal* quickly vanishes into the labyrinths of obscurity. Following the album release, Botnen retreats to his visual arts, while the Svein Finnerud Trio continue to establish themselves for years as some of the leading musicians in J&P. Throughout the 1970s, they undertake various collaborations with poets such as Magli Elster, Tor Obrestad, Einar Økland and Kate Næss, while the 1980s testify to a long, close interaction with actress Katja Medbøe.

In contrast to other countries, the production of J&P in Norway continued strongly through the 1970s. Tor Obrestad tries his hand as a *spoken word* poet in the absurd composition *Krigsmannen* (The War Man), accompanied by Finn Eriksen's orchestra on NRK radio in 1972. Even above the modern jazzfunk rhythms, Obrestad sounds as though he was born one hundred years too late as he intones about Norwegian traditional sweaters being sent back in the mail from the city to the countryside. In 1974, Gunnar Bull Gundersen continues his J&P collaboration with Bernt Brinck-Johnsen's quintet. That same year, Magli Elster is invited to write a prologue for the Molde Jazz Festival that will be performed with musicians Carl Magnus Neumann, Ole Jacob Hansen, Tarjei Venaas and Earl Wilson. Although J&P albums are released now and then on the market, the production in the radio studios and festivals is constant. Most of this broadcast material now lies deep inside climate controlled mountain storage rooms and remote storage areas where it is being preserved for posterity – and even the mountains send up a distant hurrah.

THE DAY OF THE HUMAN – BRETT BORGEN, ARNE FALCK AND WEBSTER LEWIS

One day in 1972, Arne Bendiksen is visited by actress Brett Borgen and her partner, psychiatrist and children's book author Arne Falck. They propose that Bendiksen should make a J&P album. Bendiksen is well aware that the Vold and Botnen albums have sold well, and can see the market value in the fact that Brett is the daughter of famous author Johan Borgen. He agrees to release the album. The producer, Hallvard Kvåle, who at this time was employed full time for Bendiksen, is drawn into the project. The previous year, Kvåle had recorded a double LP with the American organist Webster Lewis' quintet, titled *Webster Lewis and the Post-pop, Space-rock, Bebop, Gospel Tabernale Chorus and Orchestra Baby!* When the band comes to Oslo to work at festivals in the summer of 1972, Kvåle pulls them into the studio to lay down the background music for Brett Borgen's recitation. The resulting LP is called *Menneskedøgn* (The Day of the Human). The album fails on many levels. Brett recites theatrical poems such as *Herr. Professor, Beauracracy, When the Bomb Falls,* and *Good Day, Angst.* The whole album has the tone of a misunderstood flower child, who knows that there's grass under the asphalt, but doesn't know how to operate the drill. The music is characterized by the fact that it was played from tapes in the studio, and that the volume is lowered whenever Brett reads and fades out just after the recitation is over, even if it's mid-solo. The reception in the Norwegian press is bad, but Borgen and Falck, who see themselves as the art world's Bonnie & Clyde[53] have plans larger than the land of their birth, and record an English version called *The Day of the Human*. They make a pilgrimage to the USA to see whether they can release the album. Brett even gives a concert with the Webster Lewis quintet in an off-off-off Broadway theatre in New York, but the English version never sees the light of day. *The Day of the Human* is still residing deep in Arne Bendiksen's dusty vault.

ZAREPTA'S JAR – JENS BJØRNEBOE AND ROLF JACOBSEN

In the mid-1970s, the young singer/songwriter Ole Paus has bucks to burn, and he invests them in the record company Zarepta, apparently called after the jar of the same name (Sarepta in English). He employs Hallvard Kvåle as producer and over the next years, the label puts out everything from Radka Toneff's first album *Winter Poem* to the forbidden recording of *Yes, We Love* (the Norwegian National anthem) with Swedish jazz act Arne Domnérus. However Zareptas' first J&P album took place when the Norwegian author and poet, Jens Bjørneboe joined forces with the Swedish jazz musician Arne Domnérus, Bengt Hallberg, Rune Gustafsson, Egil Johansen, Georg Riedel and Claes Rosendahl, an orchestra that had previously been the backup band for Cornelis Vreeswijk. The album *Våpenløs* (Weaponless) is recorded in Arne Bendiksen's studio in April and May of 1976, with Ole Paus as producer. Jens Bjørneboe finds himself in the studio, but wishes he were at home at Veierland, far from the bloody city of Oslo. He is drunk, tired and unstable. Ole Paus struggles to finish the album, but tosses the author into the studio between arguments. Bjørneboe takes his own life one week after the final recording.

Whether or not one can call *Våpenløs* a J&P album is doubtful. The music feels more like a nerve-racking, medieval jester ensemble tiptoeing behind a desperate Bjørneboe throughout his poems. Each time he opens his mouth, they try to sonically translate and comment on his words, something which often ends in musical clichés and radio drama music. But despite the album's obvious weaknesses, it nonetheless has some audacious nerve. Bjørneboe is drunk and knackered in some poems, powerless and insightful in others. On a few of the tracks, Bjørneboe and the musicians come close to a common mode of expression. The cut *Natten* (The Night) opens with a percussion party and laughing roar from the author himself, and the musicians are able to find a tone to support Bjørneboe's intensity. The tune *Mitt hjerte* (My heart) is done as a demonstration of strength to a gorgeous jazz ballad. *Våpenløs* debuted in 15th place on the VG chart in 1976, and was the largest J&P commercial success in Norway since *Briskeby Blues*.

In 1976, the composer and jazz pianist Egil Kapstad hears the poet Rolf Jacobsen read his poetry on the airwaves and immediately goes about acquiring Jacobsen's poetry collections *Sommeren i gresset* (Summer in the Grass), *Til lyset* (To the Light) and *Stillheten efterpå* (The Silence Afterwards). In a chance-meeting of Kapstad with an old school mate, Johan Fredrik Heyerdahl, who at the time was the head of The Norwegian Book Club, Kapstad mentions his latest acquisition. Heyerdahl wastes no time in hustling Kapstad over to Bondeheimen, where he heard that Jacobsen is lodging. Egil Kapstad and Rolf Jacobsen quickly find their tone. Kapstad is one of the few eager poetry reading musicians within the J&P genre, and Jacobsen, though no profound jazz expert, is very open to modes of expression and eventually warms up to the music.[54] Kapstad begins traveling frequently to Hamar to visit Rolf and Petra Jacobsen, in their house that is only centimetres from the railroad tracks. They organize practice spaces in Hamar and work on a duo project, and starting small, begin to give their first performances together. They play at festivals in Harstad and Bergen, and the audience likes the whimsical combination of Rolf Jacobsen's pathos-filled voice above Kapstad's melodies. Ole Paus is attending one of the concerts, and offers to record an album on Zarepta. The duo accepts, but Kapstad wishes to expand the line up. They agree on the poems that should be on the album, and Kapstad decides to compose completely new pieces for the LP. In order to match the poetry's rhythms and increase the intensity, he hires two drummers, Ole Jacob Hansen and Svein Christiansen, in addition to the bassist Bjørn Alterhaug. Kapstad also engages a horn section consisting of Ditlef Eckhoff, Bjørn Johansen and Erik Andresen, whose job it is together to paint tonal moods before and after Jacobsen's readings, like in the sci-fi overture to the poem *Skylab.* Kapstad struggles to find poems that can be put to music and sung, the lines are too abrupt and don't fit the beat well. But one day, Jacobsen comes in with a paper on which he has scrawled a few lines in English, the poem *Big*

City. Kapstad calls up Karin Krog and convinces her to come down to the studio, and it is this melody in particular that becomes a reoccurring theme on the album. Rolf Jacobsen records his recitation of the poems first; the musicians go in directly afterward and record Kapstad's compositions. The jazz musicians and Jacobsen "jam" very little. Although the album is not as much a comprehensive whole as the J&P album *HAV*, Kapstad's patchwork is put together with great care, and Jacobsen has such an interesting voice that the album stands on its own. The resulting LP, *Til Jorden* (To the Earth) is released in 1978. On the cover of the album, Jacobsen writes:

> Poetry is language's extended arm. Ordinary prose cannot cover the whole world. Poetry attempts to push the lines a bit further out. Lyrics are an "auxilliary language" – just as music, painting and mathematics sign language. All of these "languages" help to broaden our understanding to areas where everyday alphabets fail to reach.

THE SEARCH FOR MORE THAN POPULAR MODERNISM

When Ferlinghetti and Rexroth went onstage with The Cellar Quintet, it wasn't a musical occurrence as big as that during the early days of hip-hop, when DJ Kool Herc looped the percussion break to the British band's Babe Ruth's *The Mexican* and had Coke La Rock rap on top of it. The J&P genre had the potential to become a part of popular culture, but ended up much in the same way as the *spoken word* movement in the 1990s, as a mere clause among the history of music and literature. The jazz stood too boldly on its own, the same with the literature. But even though the J&P's search for a popular modernism went awry, its basic mode of expression continued in other genres closely linked to J&P. The Afro American performers LeRoi Jones, Nikki Giovanni, The Last Poets and The Watts Prophets continued the political and musical aspects, and developed the genre more in the direction of spoken word and early rap. Poetry's entry into show business was rather realised through the singer/songwriter movement and the broadside ballad tradition, from Bob Dylan to Cornelis Vreeswijk.

Norway is one of few countries in which the J&P genre enjoyed a wide and continuous relevance, even until today. It is significant that almost all of our largest post-war poets flirted with the genre. Important contributing factors to this were of course that large portions of the Norwegian poetry scene, in particular within the Profile-circles, were very fond of American beat culture and immediately adopted J&P in Norway. At the same time, the culture of poetry readings was quite strong in Norway at this time, and was a stable form of income for poets. Throughout the 1960s and 1970s, jazz developed as the musical genre in which Norway distinguished itself internationally, and was therefore also popular. A particular hallmark of the Norwegian J&P scene is that it was our foremost musicians and poets who collaborated, in contrast to other countries where such cooperations were less equally distributed. This has led to a balance of understanding, ambition and expression and has allowed for a thoroughly high quality in production. Vold and Garbarek's albums are some of the best of their kind even internationally, and these long lasting, professional collaborations lay the foundation for new generations of musicians and poets together. Throughout the 1980s and 90s, the symbiosis between words and music in Norway was further developed by authors like Olav Angell, Arild Nyquist, Lars Saabye Christensen and Øyvind Berg. Some may claim that slam poetry is the way forward, but that discussion should rather take place somewhere else, some other time – best in the presence of security guards.

BREAST IS BEST

And then you become a father. New Norwegian abstract art is replaced by studies of shadows, colour gradations and amoeba-like patterns in diapers. The dream of standing outside on a cold autumn night, clothed in a warm jacket, stargazing, brimming with wonder, honour and calm – is far less appealing than observing a child's toothless scream.

Gleaning wisdom from friends, whose lives are lived to the soundtracks of Elmo and Fireman Sam, I've decided to purchase the American avant-gardist Raymond Scott's *Soothing Sounds for Baby* from 1963. Across the cover of the LP is the slogan: *An Infant's Friend in Sound,* advertising that the music provides an: "aid to the mother during breast-feeding, teething, playing, sleep and baby's uneasy periods." Before me lays our test specimen: Gudbrand, 3 weeks old. Based on the creature's angst-ridden face, it appears he strongly disapproves of the spread of milky gasses throughout his intestines, which occurs when one is out to double one's body weight in six weeks' time. We hope that the album makes good on its promises.

Raymond Scott (1908—1994) made a name for himself as a hit composer, jazz musician and big band leader in the USA in the 1930s. He led the Raymond Scott Quintette and CBS Jazz Big Band, released some frightening concept albums such as *At Home with Dorothy Collins* and *Ectoplasm*, and wrote the soundtracks for Bugs Bunny and Daffy Duck cartoons. Despite his upward career trajectory, in the 1940s he began to pull back into the laboratory to cultivate his interest in electronics. He established the *Manhattan Research Inc* – at which Robert Moog was the errand boy – to develop new instruments such as Clavivox, Electronium and the drum machine Bandito The Bongo Artist. Scott's music from this period most often ends up in the *Exotica* section of record stores or in the half-dollar piles next to opera and Christian LPs, but it could also be classified under avant garde and contemporary music. Run and search on Spotify or Apple Music for the song *Lightworks*, the perfect hybrid of pop sensibility and experimental electronic music.

Soothing Sounds for Baby was published in collaboration with the Gesell Institute for Child Development INC, an idealistic non-profit organisation in Connecticut dedicated to research on the growth and development of children. Gesell's employees discovered that babies could hear much better than previously thought, and they therefore wished to develop a scientific method of creating music to sooth infants – a pedagogical sound toy. The researchers believed that babies "like new sounds and sights" and that repetitive and simple music could stimulate them. Based on this knowledge, Raymond Scott was invited to compose minimalistic rhythmical music, often arranged around a sweet lullaby. In order to live up to its "new sounds" claim, he created all of the music on his electronic equipment. In spite of titles such as *Sleepy Time* and *Little Miss Echo*, not one single baby was ever calmed down, and today the music is safely piled onto the scrapheap of child pedagogy, alongside Benjamin Spock and Bill Cosby's *Fatherhood*. However, in later years the recordings were recalled from the archives and are today viewed as the forerunners to ambient music – released ten years before Brian Eno had similar ideas.

Let us try out the album on Gudbrand. I place the needle on the opening tune *Lullaby*, but Gudbrand looks out the window and focuses on the play of light through the trees – does he even register the music at all? The next track is *Sleepy Time*. Papa holds still as a mouse so that Gudbrand can focus on the sounds, and I fall into daydreams about Scott and his laboratory.

Waaaaaeeeeeee! Aaarraaaahhhh! It's obvious he's had enough of Raymond's Scott's experimentation. He screeches at me: listening to *Soothing Sounds for Baby* is like chewing on terracotta! Mama comes in, glances in exasperation over at the torturer as she folds down her nursing bra. The room changes from a complete cacophony to utter silence. The results of the experiment are as follows: Raymond Scott is suited to dance music for adults, but is unhelpful for breaking in newborns. La Leche League is spot-on forever: breast is best.

THE LAST RAZORBILL

The opening scene in Jan Horne's film *Norwegian Artists in the 1960s* takes one's breath away. The roadway and pavement at the intersection of Inkognito street and Meltzers street in Oslo is besieged by sculptures of glass, metal and polyester. To a dizzyingly electronic soundtrack, artist Marius Heyerdahl appears to be aching for a brawl; he trips, dances, stretches out his joints and punches the air. As random passersby stare down at the asphalt, Heyerdahl casts a scornful glance on his artwork before laying down in the middle of the street for a snooze. The entire scenario brings to mind a scene from *Raging Bull*, and Marius Heyerdahl appears just as rootless and reckless as a Robert de Niro. One catches a glimpse of fellow artist Per Kleiva slinking around in the background, ready to send his protégé out into the ring. Heyerdahl boxes out of his corner, sticks his head into a metal sculpture and screams noiselessly into the camera.

Marius Heyerdahl (1938—1979) entered the Norwegian art scene as an outsider in the early 1960s. With artist Teddy Røwde as his mother and sociologist Arvid Brodersen as his stepfather, Heyerdahl had an international orientation since childhood. He had worked in Asia and Africa, learned five languages and studied art at the University of California, Berkeley and Arts Students League in New York in the 1950s. In 1964, he debuted at Wangs Kunsthandel in Oslo with paintings such as *Nymphomania Blues* and *Angrende Selvmorder* (Reluctant Suicidal), clearly inspired by Willem de Kooning and Robert Motherwell, as well as by the howl of beat poetry. In the same year, Heyerdahl participated in the exhibition *Noen unge refuserte* (Some Young Rejects) at which he read aloud from a self-authored manifesto that praised the use of everyday objects in art: "Isn't there just as much beauty in the body of a flying machine or a can of coke, as in many so-called acknowledged sculptures?" Over the next three years, Heyerdahl would come to embody these words in three radical sound sculptures.

At the Autumn Exhibition (Høstutstillingen) in 1965, Heyerdahl presented *Homo Cyberneticus 1 & 2*. The two robots were built from parts of modified washing machines, cash registers, radios and high voltage insulators. If one were to plug into an outlet, they started to spin and flash and sound emanated out. *HC 1 & 2* were only accepted at the mercy of the jury after one member, Arnold Haukeland, argued that the work could be called sculpture. Flummoxed by their own decision, the jury placed the robots at the top of the stairway at Kunstnernes Hus, in between the hall for paintings and the hall for sculptures, as though to show that they did not belong anywhere – in retrospect a step-motherly treatment of Norway's first kinetic sculpture and sound art piece.

The following year, Heyerdahl exhibited *Herold* in Lektorenes Hus, right next to Kunstnernes Hus. The work was comprised of a ship valve containing a concealed compressed air flute inside. Like a step child of Luigi Russolo's futuristic instruments, the maritime readymade *Herold* stood piping out a middle finger in the direction of the Autumn Exhibition that had forced him to flounder in a no-man's-land earlier that year. For his next work, Heyerdahl travelled to a slaughterhouse where he was able to get the skeleton of a cow. Back at his atelier, he painted the cadaver silver and mounted it on a metal bar in a posture which looked as though it had been either crucified or ready to attack the viewer. To achieve an even more dreadful impression, Heyerdahl positioned red lights in the cow's empty eye sockets and loud speakers in its "palms". At UKS (Young Artists Association) in 1966, the sound sculpture *Lucifer* snarled at the public – as one of the oddest and most ground-breaking artworks created in Norway in the post-war years.

In the 1970s, Heyerdahl's focus turned toward environmental activism and more traditional sculptures, but he continued to carry a vision to create sound sculptures for public space. These creations – that looked like a blend between Robert Jacobsen's metal constructions and Alexander Calder's mobiles – were to be played on by children and citizens with hands and mallets and provide an interactive soundtrack to everyday life. None of his works were ever realised.

The attentive reader may have noticed within the contents of this text about sound art, there is not a single description of sound. There is unfortunately a simple explanation for this. In 1979, Marius Heyerdahl took his own life, beforehand tossing most of his work into the sea. Given Heyerdahl's unique position as a pioneer within environmental activism and sound art, one can only hope that someone will take responsibility for writing a book or presenting a retrospective exhibition dedicated to this strange bird amongst Norwegian fauna.

ALL THAT'S NEW BEGINS IN CHAOS

December is the high season for rural racism. In one broad sweep, comparable only to the strain experienced by the Chinese transportation system around May 1st, prodigal Norwegian children travel away from Oslo back to their childhood rooms in Mysen and Hamar. By the time Christmas Eve rolls around, the population of the capital city has been reduced by 80% and Oslo looks like a theatre set ready for demolition. And as the Christmas wrapping crackles and emits poisonous gases within the wood stove for young and old alike, and dad screams out "deprivation of liberty!" to mum for forbidding him the opportunity to watch a YouTube video clip of an ape during Christmas preparations. Oslo's lonesome souls slink out to the slum boroughs to the only two bars that remain open: Palace Grill and London Pub.

And it was to this gathering of fathers with no custody rights, vagrants, secular migrants and people with fossil parents who turn in at 11 p.m. that two small gangsters went astray. John Cale had to be replaced by Akon, and after a scuffle with the bartender that escalated for 45 minutes, one of them threatened loudly: "I have pistols hidden in bushes all around Oslo. I'll be back!" Without knowing it, he had spoken the magical words which unleashed the entire latent protestant aggression that had been pent up in the locale, and dozens of women and men flew off to make raspberry jam with their faces as ingredients. He and his mate ran out to their Mercedes, while we stayed together with John Cale, glancing out of the window, and waiting.

But now I have to rest my mouth a bit. There was another experience I wanted to share, namely the Norwegian theatre and art collective Verdensteatret's work *Bridge Over Mud* (Broen over Gjørme) that was shown at the Ultima Festival in 2014. Because it is a truth generally acknowledged that Verdensteatret's art cannot be described in words, and since there's a chance of being labelled as *reciprocal masturbation* when the original premiere was unveiled at my own workplace, I will attempt to be as dry as possible. In January of 2013, Verdensteatret came up with the idea of holding a large retrospective exhibition at the Henie Onstad Kunstsenter. They wished to show installation versions of old works side by side with their new, still untitled works. Unfortunately it didn't happen. In March 2014, an email from VT's founder, Lisbeth Bodd spoke of large reorganisations. She had been taken ill and had cancelled the planned world tour. Could we meet at their workshop at Kampen and talk about doing something with Ultima?

We didn't hear anything from VT throughout the summer. They entered into a collective trauma in order to complete the work. When the rigging began at Henie Onstad in August, it was done according to the *before-the-curator-took-over-principle:* "Here's the key to the hall, good luck." The few times that I peeked in through the door, it felt like observing an elven workshop on December 23rd, a CERN laboratory and a crafty band of felons planning the perfect heist. I saw kinetic bird robots, speaker horns from Vietnam, fake walls, dozens of meters worth of toy train tracks, gleaming tubas, mobile magnifying glasses, projectors and fraught nerves: All that's new begins in chaos.

Bridge Over Mud was unveiled on September 19th; it was a work so flawless in its chaos that the programme should have warned "Use sparingly." What else can one say about sound and images that gives one the feeling of detention, the tip of your tongue on a battery, wingspan, that the metal joints along Norwegian roadways are not there because the asphalt expands with shifts in temperature but rather are a dangerous military tool employed by the administration, the abominable snowman, not dropping off my father's corpse to the medical office when (if) he dies, that interpretation is the intellect's revenge on art, and a galloping race horse that, rather than breaking through the velvet ribbon at the finishing line instead runs straight into an open razor blade and is sliced in half as its legs continue to run – all of this in the course of 45 minutes? Lisbeth was at the opening. She was able to experience that it went well. A few hours after the last performance of *Bridge Over Mud* on September 28, she passed away.

Back to the slum borough. No one ever returned with an automatic pistol. We listened to Phil Spector's Christmas album until closing time and scratched at our beards: perhaps his gun had rusted or the gunpowder had gotten damp from lying behind a bush in Oslo in the winter? Maybe a homeless person had found it and hung it over the fire-place? Or, to try believing in the good in people – he had mended his ways.

NOTES

1 Morton Feldman interviewed in *A John Cage Reader: In Celebration of His 70th Birthday*, Ed. Peter Gena og Jonathan Brent (London: C. F. Peters, 1982)

2 John Dewey, *Art as Experience.* (New York: Perigee Trade, 1959)

3 John Cage, *Silence.* (Middeltown: Wesleyan University Press, 1961)

4 John Cage in the liner notes for *Indeterminacy – New Aspect of Form in Instrumental and Electronic Music.* (Washington: Folkways Records, 1959)

5 John Cage in the liner notes for *Indeterminacy – New Aspect of Form in Instrumental and Electronic Music.* (Washington: Folkways Records, 1959)

6 John Cage, *Empty Words Writings '73—'78.* (Middeltown: Wesleyan University Press, 1979)

7 Edwin Orr Denby (b. 4th of February 1903, d. 12th of July 1983) American writer, poet, translator and dance critic for Herald Tribune

8 Jackson Mac Low (f. 12th of September 1922, d. 8th of December 2004): American poet, translator, composer and performance artist. Studied experimental composition under Cage at The New School in New York in the 50s. Mac Lows form of poetry, vocabularies, was a source of inspiration for Cage's mesostics.

9 IC can be downloaded here: www.newmus.net/filelib.html

10 www.newyorkmyc.org

11 John Cage, Lois Long & Alexander Smith, *The Mushroom Book.* (New York: Hollanders Workshop, 1972)

12 John Cage, *For The Birds – JOHN CAGE in conversation with Daniel Charles.* (London: Marion Boyars Inc, 1981)

13 John Cage, *anarchy.* (Middeltown: Wesleyan University Press, 1988)

14 Terje Mosnes, «Happy New Ears», *Dagbladet,* 10. November 1983.

15 John Cage, *Preface to Lecture on the Weather.* (New York: Henmar Press, 1975)

16 John Cage, «Seriously Comma» i *A Year From Monday – New Lectures and Writings* (Middeltown: Wesleyan University Press, 1967)

17 The term is often attributed to either the founder of the Salvation Army, William Boothe (1829—1912), or the founder of the Methodist Church, John Wesley (1703—1791). The Christian rock star Larry Norman popularised the expression with his hit song from 1972 *Why Should the Devil Have All the Good Music?*

18 Robert W. Kvalvaag, *The Eleventh Commandment* (Oslo: Unipub, 2011)

19 Robert W. Kvalvaag, *The Eleventh Commandment* (Oslo: Unipub, 2011)

20 From the inlay card of *Lukk opp kirkens dører* (Open Up the Doors of the Church), (Oslo: For-X LP1, 1974)

21 Geir Lie, *Norsk Jesusbevegelse et historisk overblikk* (Norwegian Jesus Movement – A Historical Overview), *Ung Teologi,* 2003

22 Note written by Bjørn Fongaard in New York, 1952. From Bjørn Fongaard's private archive, Larvik, 2011.

23 Note written by Bjørn Fongaard, 1948. From Bjørn Fongaard's private archive, Larvik, 2011.

24 Fongaard interviewed by Knut Høyland in *Programbladet,* 1979

25 Fongaard interviewed by Knut Høyland in *Programbladet,* 1979

26 Fongaard interviewed by Vibeke Otto in *Programbladet,* 1972

27 Fongaard interviewed by Vibeke Otto in *Programbladet,* 1972

28 Fongaard interviewed by Knut Høyland in *Programbladet,* 1979

29 Fongaard quote taken from the NRK TV programme *Komponist med gitar.* Broadcast 13.03.1971

30 Note written by Bjørn Fongaard, unknown date. From Bjørn Fongaard's private archive, Larvik, 2011.

31 Note written by Bjørn Fongaard, 1963. From Bjørn Fongaard's private archive, Larvik, 2011.

32 Walter Baumgartner, "Jazz och poesi i Samspel," in *Intermedialitet,* ed. Hans Lund (Lund: Studentlitteratur, 2002)

33 ibid.

34 Quote taken from Ralph J. Gleason's cover text on *Poetry Readings in "The Cellar"* (San Francisco: Fantasy Records, 1957).

35 Lonnie Elder & Charles Mingus, *A Modern Jazz Symposium of Music and Poetry.* (New York: Bethlehem Records, 1957).

36 Jack Kerouac & Steve Allen, *Poetry for the Beat Generation.* (New York: Dot Records, 1958).

37 Langston Hughes, Red Allen, Charles Mingus & Leonard Feather, *Weary Blues.* (New York: Verve, 1958).

38 Kenneth Rexroth, Lawrence Ferlinghetti & The Cellar Quintet, *Poetry Readings in the Cellar.* (San Francisco: Fantasy Records, 1957).

39 Jan Erik Vold, "Kammer og jazz konsert", *Dagbladet,* February 23, 1960.

40 It is not clear who were members of the band, but Hans Marius Stormoen, Peter Holm, Ole Jacob Hansen, Per Løberg and Jon Christensen were all involved at various times.

41 Stein Mehren remarked in a conversation with the author, Lars Mørch Finborud on February 5, 2008, that he didn't find the whole thing so meaningful, and jumped off of the P&J bandwagon early on, as he didn't find American culture as interesting as some of the others, but rather adhered to the more German and British brands of intellectual life.

42 Åkesson had himself recorded the poem *Sjölvbiografi (Autobiography)* in 1966 on a vinyl single with the trumpet player Jan Allen, inserted into the poetry collection *Jag bor i Sverige* (I live in Sweden). (Stockholm: Rabén & Sjögren, 1966).

43 Jan Erik Vold in a conversation with Lars Mørch Finborud, Oslo, December 7, 2007.

44 Jan Erik Vold, *Dagbladet,* February 1, 1959.

45 Jan Erik Vold, *Dagbladet,* June 29, 1960.

46 Jan Erik Vold, *Profil,* nr. 2, 1962.

47 Jan Erik Vold, *Dagbladet,* March 14, 1964.

48 *Magasinet For Alle,* September 1970.

49 *Dagbladet,* November 17, 1970.

50 Jan Erik Vold "På med ørene!" *Programme flyer,* January 27, 1971.

51 Excerpt from the programme flyer for the National Concerts *Multimal* tour in 1971.

52 Eivind Kahrs recited Trond Botnen's poem on this tour, when Botnen prioritized to do an exhibition instead.

53 Brett Borgen in conversation with Lars Mørch Finborud, Oslo, March 12, 2004.

54 Egil Kapstad in conversation with Lars Mørch Finborud, Oslo, February 7, 2008.

Sanding Down Gravestones

Lars Mørch Finborud

A Broken Dimanche Press Publication

Berlin, Germany, 2017

www.brokendimanche.eu

ISBN: 978-3-943196-44-3

Design: Form und Konzept (www.formundkonzept.de)

Translation: Becky L. Crook (except * by John Holten & Associates)

This translation has been published with the financial support of NORLA

Copy-editing: John Holten and Lars Mørch Finborud

Author photo: Anniken C. Mohr

Printed at: Opolgraf, Poland (www.opolgraf.com.pl)

Broken Dimanche Press

Büro BDP

Mareschstrasse 1

D-12055 Berlin